US Airborne Tanks, 1939–1945

US Airborne Tanks, 1939–1945

CHARLES C. ROBERTS, JR

FRONTLINE
BOOKS

US AIRBORNE TANKS, 1939–1945

First published in Great Britain in 2021
and reissued in this format in 2025 by
Frontline Books
An imprint of
Pen & Sword Books Ltd
Yorkshire – Philadelphia

ISBN 978 1 52679 865 7

A CIP catalogue record for this book is available from the British Library

Typeset in 10.5/13 pt Palatino
by SJmagic DESIGN SERVICES, India.
Printed and bound in the UK by TJ Books Ltd.

MIX
Paper | Supporting responsible forestry
FSC® C013604

The Publisher's authorised representative in the EU for product safety is Authorised Rep Compliance Ltd., Ground Floor, 71 Lower Baggot Street, Dublin D02 P593, Ireland.
www.arccompliance.com

For a complete list of Pen & Sword titles please contact

PEN & SWORD BOOKS LTD
47 Church Street, Barnsley, South Yorkshire, S70 2AS, England

E-mail: enquiries@pen-and-sword.co.uk
Website: www.pen-and-sword.co.uk
or
PEN AND SWORD BOOKS
1950 Lawrence Road, Havertown, PA 19083, USA
E-mail: uspen-and-sword@casematepublishers.com
Website: www.penandswordbooks.com

SC C

Contents

Acknowledgements and Picture Credits

A special thanks to Lydia Roberts, Michael Krizsanitz, Jeff Wszolek, Patrick Tipton, Dave Kaufman and Lester Hughes for their invaluable help in editing and researching various aspects of this book.

The following abbreviations have been used in the picture credits in the captions:

The American Society of Military Insignia Collectors – The American Society of Military Insignia Collectors, Trading Post, April–June 2001

Chamberlain and Pugh, *T.3 Christie* – P. Chamberlain and S. Pugh, *T.3 Christie,* Armor in Profile, Profile Publications Ltd, Great Bookham, 1967

https://ww2db.com – GAL 49 Hamilcar, 17 October 2019

FM 17-12, *Armored Force Field Manual, Tank Gunnery* – FM 17-12, *Armored Force Field Manual, Tank Gunnery,* War Department, 22 April 1943

FM 17-15, *Armored Force Field Manual, Combat Practice Firing Armored Force Units* – FM 17-15, *Armored Force Field Manual, Combat Practice Firing Armored Force Units,* 15 May 1942

FM 23-81, *Basic Field Manual 37-MM Gun, Tank M6 (Mounted in Tanks)* – FM 23-81, *Basic Field Manual 37-MM Gun, Tank M6 (Mounted in Tanks),* War Department, 3 April 1942

General Motors Proving Grounds – General Motors Proving Grounds, Milford, Michigan http://www.historyofwar.org/Pictures/pictures_m22_locust_hamilcar.html – J. Rickard (24 February 2014), M22 Light tank 'Locust' in Hamilcar glider, http:// www.historyofwar.org/Pictures/pictures_m22_locust_hamilcar.html

IBCC Digital Archive – 'Halifax towing Hamilcar glider', IBCC Digital Archive, accessed 6 January 2020, https:// ibccdigitalarchive.lincoln.ac.uk/omeka/collections/document/383

Kolomiets, *Tanki-amfibii T-37, T-38, T-40* – M. Kolomiets, *Tanki-amfibii T-37, T-38, T-40*, Frontovaya Illustratsiya/Frontline Illustration, 3/2003, Moscow

Hughes, 'The 151st Airborne Tank Company' – Lester Hughes, 'The 151st Airborne Tank Company', Trading Post, July–September 1987

Lycoming Model O-435-A Aviation Engine Manual – *Lycoming Model O-435-A Aviation Engine Manual*, Lycoming-Spenser, Williamsport, PA

Marmon-Herrington Company – Marmon-Herrington Company, 13001 Magisterial Drive Louisville, Kentucky 40223

Modern Mechanics and Inventions, Vol. VIII – *Modern Mechanics and Inventions*, Vol. VIII, Number 3, July 1932, Fawcett Publications, Inc., Minneapolis, Minnesota

Popular Mechanics, Vol. 58 – *Popular Mechanics*, Vol. 58, Number 1, July 1932

Popular Mechanics, Vol. 65 – *Popular Mechanics*, Vol. 65, Number 5, May 1936

http://www.ww2incolor.com – public domain photographs, 21 August 2019

Sacquety, 'The 151st Airborne Tank Company at Camp Mackall, NC' – Troy Sacquety, 'The 151st Airborne Tank Company at Camp Mackall, NC', *Veritas: Journal of Army Special Operations History* 3, no. 3:23–30, 2007

Stanton, *Order of Battle: U.S. Army, World War II* – S.L. Stanton *Order of Battle: U.S. Army, World War II*, Presidio Press, 1984

T-315, *Combat Orders* – T-315, *Combat Orders*, Tactics Department, Armored Force School, Fort Knox, November 1942

T37-A Soviet Amphibious Tank – Case Report – *T37-A Soviet Amphibious Tank – Case Report*, September 15, 2019, http://panzerserra.blogspot.com/

https://commons.wikimedia.org/wiki/Commons – Wikimedia Commons, 21 August 2019

TM 9-724, *Light Tank T-9E1* – TM 9-724, *Light Tank T-9E1*, War Department, 17 November 1943

TM9-1907, *Ballistic Data Performance of Ammunition* – TM9-1907, *Ballistic Data Performance of Ammunition*, War Department, 23 September 1944

TM 11-2705, *Installation of Radio and Interphone Equipment in Light Tank T-9E1* – TM 11-2705, *Installation of Radio and Interphone Equipment in Light Tank T-9E1*, War Department, 13 April 1944

US Army Report – US Army Report of Combined Airborne-Troop Carrier Maneuver, 24–9 September 1944

Author's Note

Every effort has been made to contact the copyright holders of the images used in this book. However, the sources in some cases are varied or obscure, in which instances the author would welcome, via the publisher, any information that would allow a full acknowledgement to be made.

Introduction

The development of airborne operations started in the 1930s in many countries. The doctrine was to deliver troops by glider or parachute ahead of an attack and behind enemy lines to disrupt defensive operations and counter-attacks. Because of limitations on the weight of the cargo an aircraft could transport, airborne soldiers were lightly armed, making them vulnerable to enemy fire. Consequently, it was thought that providing armored vehicles with more substantial armament that could be delivered by air would help offset this disparity between the firepower of airborne troops and enemy defenders. The problem was how to deliver such heavy equipment to a landing strip or drop zone.

The first airborne tank design was initiated by renowned tank designer Walter Christie. He envisioned a light-weight armored vehicle hull with a powerful engine with a power take-off unit that would drive a propeller. Lift was provided by wings attached to the armored vehicle hull. Work on a prototype began, but the project was never completed due to financial constraints. However, several countries incorporated elements of the armored vehicle's suspension into their own designs. The Russians experimented with slinging a small tank to the underbelly of a large aircraft. This was problematic in that the aircraft had to land in order to deploy the armored vehicle. This, in turn, required that an airfield suitable for the landing and take-off of a large aircraft be available for use behind enemy lines. The Russians also experimented with the design of tank to which a glide wing was attached, allowing the tank to be towed by an aircraft and then released for landing at a battlefield. This also proved impractical. These efforts utilized small tanks that were not designed for airborne operation. The Germans were delivering armored vehicles utilizing the Gigant aircraft to a combat area, but rarely to a battlefield. The Japanese experimented with a large glider (Ku-7), but few were built and none were used in combat.

The first serious effort to aerial deliver armor to the battlefield was by the British. The Tetrarch light tank, which was not designed to be an airborne tank, was coupled with the large Hamilcar glider and used in Operation Overlord and Operation Market Garden. The British were influential in the development of the first operational light tank (M22 Locust) designed for airborne transport by the United States. The US Army could not come up with a practical means of delivering the tank to the battlefield so the M22 was relegated to training and was not used with US forces in combat. The British were able to deliver the M22 by Hamilcar glider in Operation Varsity, when it was used with moderate success.

Airborne armored vehicle usage in the Second World War suffered from the lack of feasible delivery methods. This stimulated the development of aircraft and armor suitable for aerial delivery to the battlefield. This book details the usage and attempted usage of airborne armored vehicles on the battlefield in the Second World War.

Chapter 1

The Airborne Tank Concept

Walter Christie was an engineer with experience in designing race cars and other unique vehicles. During the First World War, he developed a prototype wheeled gun carriage for the US Army. The Ordnance Board had certain specifications for an airborne armored vehicle, which did not conform to Christie's idea of what a military vehicle should look like. He refused to alter his designs to match these military specifications and engaged in disagreements with the Ordnance Board, which essentially killed his project with the Army. In 1928, Christie patented a suspension system for tanks that was revolutionary. It involved independent road wheels using a control arm and spring system for each wheel, which resulted in very high-speed cross-country mobility. There were no support rollers for the track since the road wheels were large and supported the track at the top of each wheel. A tank using this system was called the model 1928. The tracks were removable so that the tank could travel on the large road wheels at high speed. The armor on the tank was thin and sloped, thus deflecting only small projectiles, such as those fired by infantry rifles.

The Christie suspension was an innovation for its time in that each road wheel of the tracked vehicle absorbed terrain variations independently of the other wheels, resulting in a smoother and faster ride. The wheel was large enough to act as the return roller for the track. When the track was removed, the larger wheels gave good road performance at high speeds on both prepared and unprepared roadways. One problem with the design was the space required for the coil springs. Later tank designs looked similar to Christie's but used a torsion bar in place of a spring. The torsion bar would be mounted at the bottom of the hull, taking up less space.

In 1932, Christie produced a prototype airborne tank, as seen on p. 6. It was technically not a tank but an armored assault vehicle, since it did not have a rotating turret. The accepted definition of a tank is an armored tracked vehicle with a rotating turret, with the crew fully enclosed. Despite this, it is typically referred to as the Christie airborne tank. It carried one 75mm gun and several machine guns. The armor was 0.375- to 0.5in-thick steel plate. Maximum speed was 60mph on track, and 120mph with the tracks removed and stored on the vehicle. The suspension conformed to the patent with aluminum wheels and pneumatic tires developed by the Firestone Tire and Rubber Company. The length of

Above: A Christie T-3 tank model 1931 delivered to the US Army for evaluation. (Chamberlain and Pugh, *T.3 Christie*)

Opposite: The 1931 patent of the Christie suspension system. This was a revolutionary design that was copied, fully or partially, by many countries. This allowed for high speed and good ride over rough terrain capability. This also significantly improved the feasibility of an airborne tank since it could travel at high speed without the tracks attached, which could be installed after landing.(US Patent Office, patent number 1,836,446)

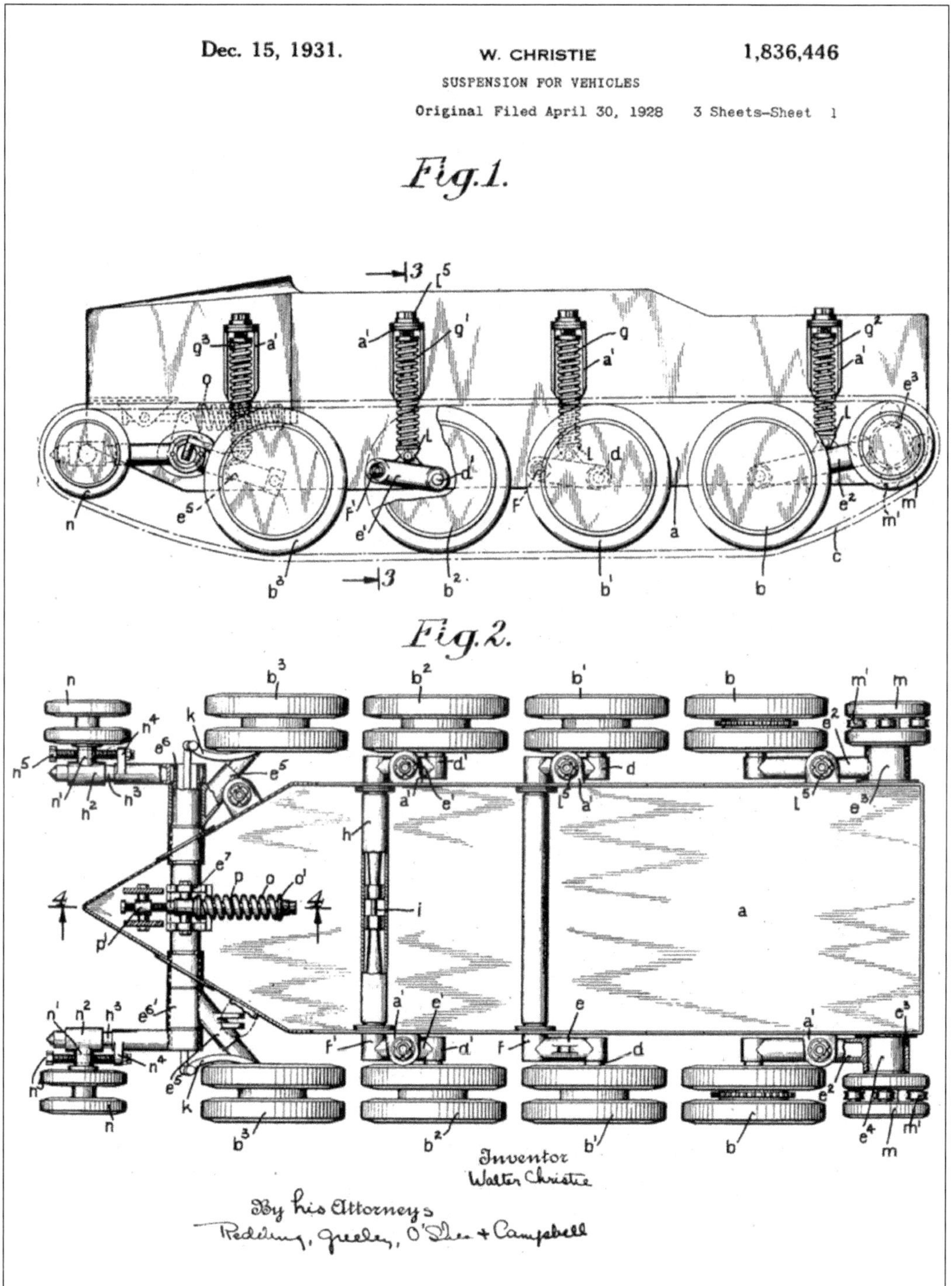
Dec. 15, 1931.
W. CHRISTIE
1,836,446
SUSPENSION FOR VEHICLES
Original Filed April 30, 1928
3 Sheets-Sheet 1
Fig.1.
Fig.2.
Inventor
Walter Christie
By his Attorneys
Redding, Greeley, O'Shea & Campbell

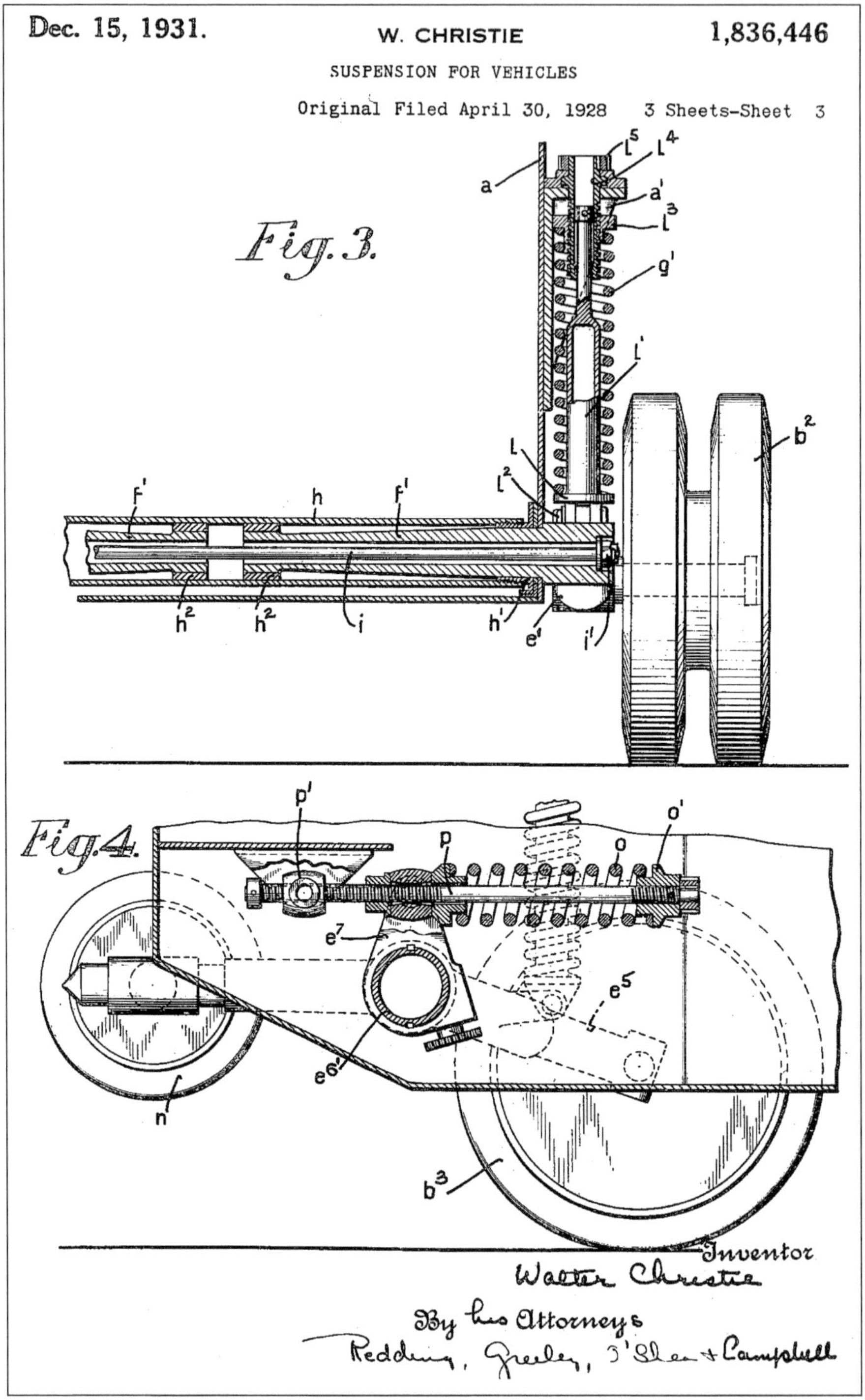
Dec. 15, 1931.
W. CHRISTIE
1,836,446
SUSPENSION FOR VEHICLES
Original Filed April 30, 1928 3 Sheets-Sheet 3
Fig. 3.
Fig. 4.
Inventor
Walter Christie
By his Attorneys
Redding, Greeley, O'Shea + Campbell

Opposite: A detailed view of the Christie suspension system. The top drawing describes the suspension system for the road wheels on each side of the vehicle. The bottom drawing describes the suspension system for the front of the vehicle which controls track tension. (US Patent Office, patent number 1,836,446)

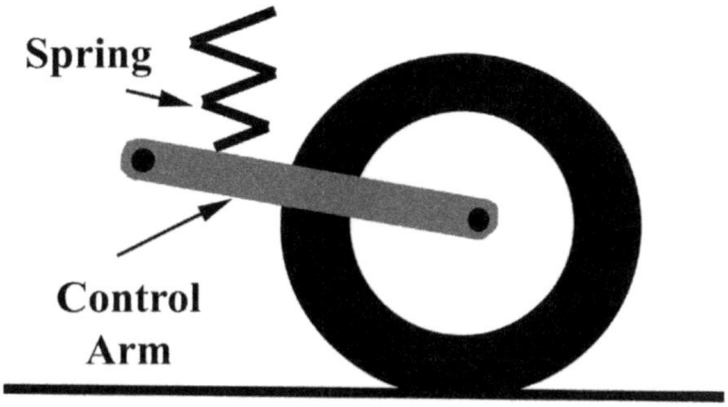

Right: A simplified drawing of the Christie suspension system. The control arm moves up and down to absorb irregularities in the terrain.

Below: The Christie-designed airborne armored car M-1933. (Chamberlain and Pugh, *T.3 Christie*)

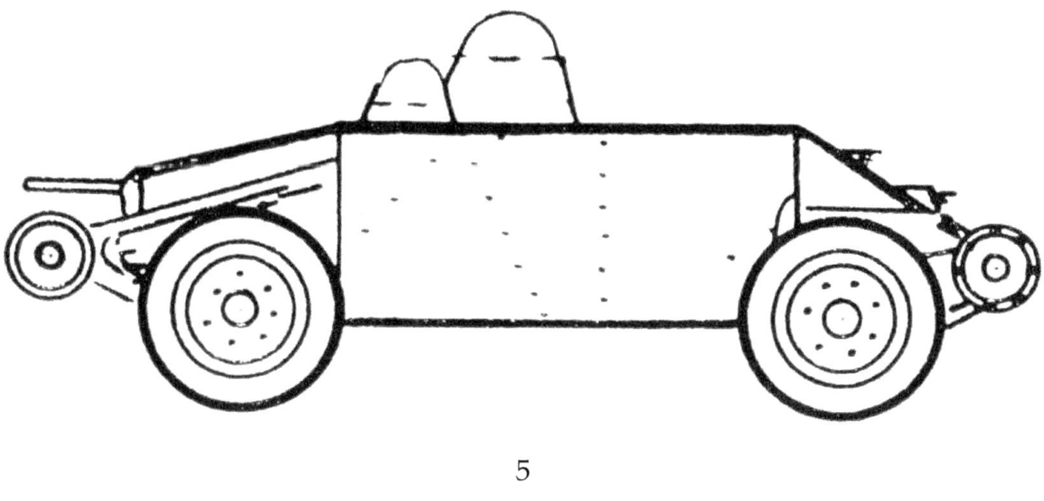

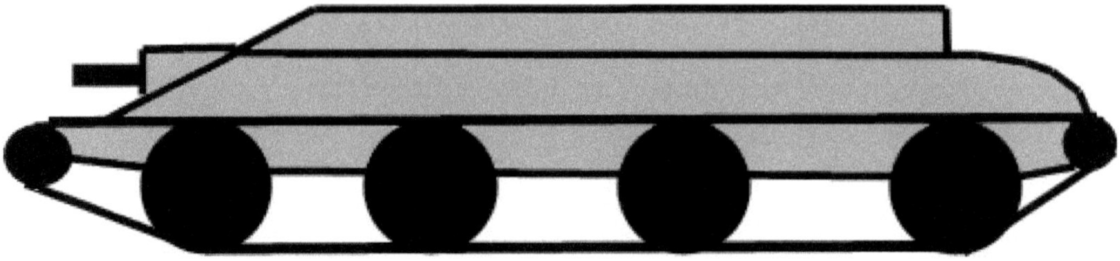

The Walter Christie-designed M1932 airborne tank produced by the Wheel Track Layer Corporation. (Chamberlain and Pugh, *T.3 Christie*)

the Christie prototype was 22ft, width 7ft and height about 5ft 8in. The engine was a V12 rated at 750HP. Weight was approximately 5 tons. The transmission had three forward gears and one reverse as well as a power take-off unit for a propeller used by the airplane wing attachment. Fuel capacity was 89 gallons. The main structure of the vehicle was a double hull. The inner hull had aluminum plates and the outer hull had steel plates. The aluminum plates, which significantly reduced the weight of the vehicle, were a source of concern for the US military, which believed they were too thin. The rear road wheels were powered to propel the vehicle when the tracks were stored. The detachable biplane assembly was used for independent flight operation. The unit was designed to taxi to the runway and accelerate to take-off speed using the road wheels. As the flying 'tank' began to lift, the propeller would take over and the unit would become airborne. The driver/pilot would guide the aircraft to the landing zone, accelerate the wheels or tracks to the proper landing speed, land, detach the biplane assembly and proceed to the battle area. The wings would then be picked up for possible future use.

The US Army purchased several Christie tank prototypes for testing. The Tank Board wanted tanks with significant armor at the expense of mobility. Christie argued for thinner armor and high speed. This disagreement resulted in the US Army never adopting these designs. Christie, upset with the rejection of his designs by his own government, started peddling his ideas to the Russians, the British and the Polish, despite not having approval from the State Department to do so. Christie continued work on new designs which led to the airborne tank in 1932.

Christie envisioned a flying tank that flew on its own power. A 1000HP engine would not only drive the tank wheels but also drive a propeller through a power take-off mechanism. The drawings below and on the next page illustrate the concept. The armored vehicle, not

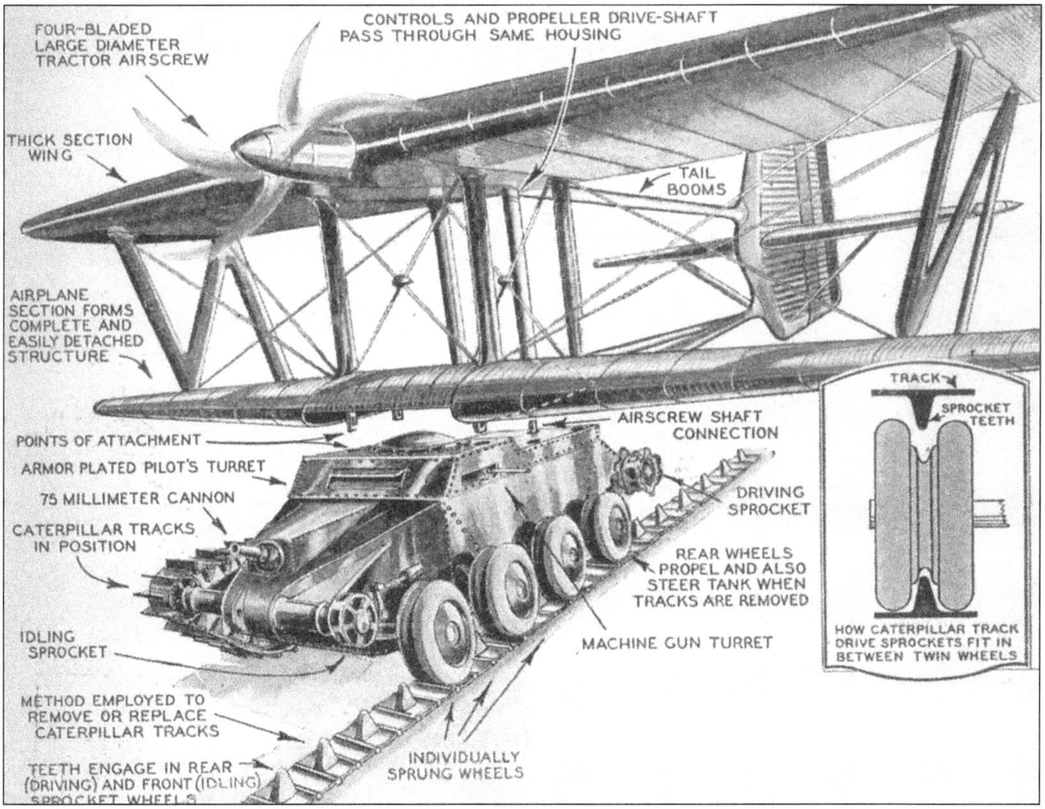

Above and overleaf: Christie's concept of the powered airborne tank. (*Modern Mechanics and Inventions*, Vol. VIII)

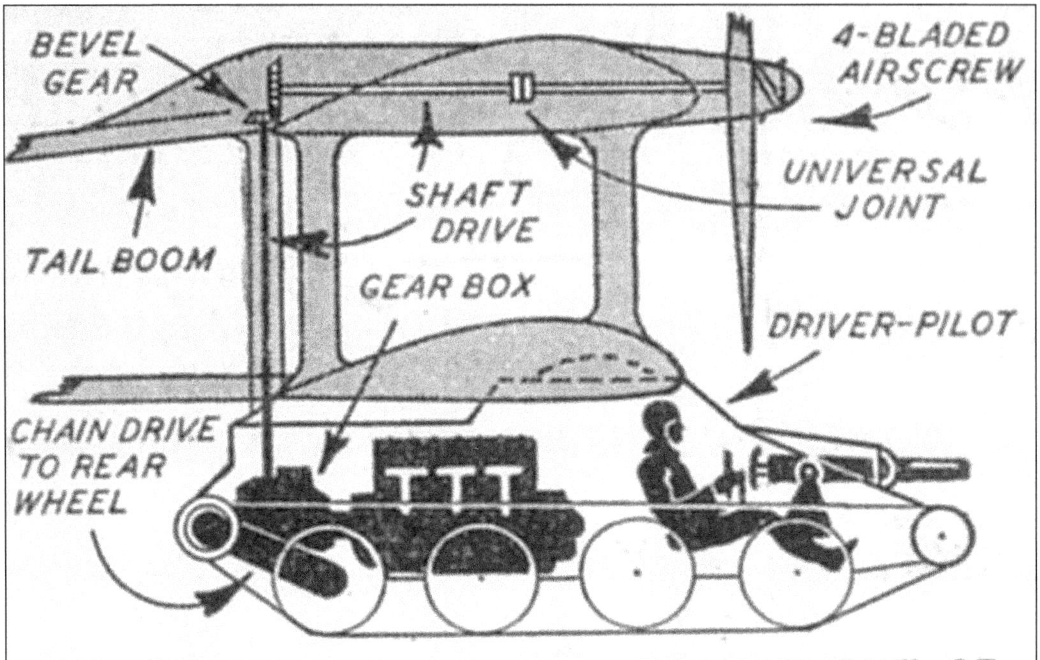

SIDE ELEVATION SHOWING ARRANGEMENT OF THE POWER DRIVE TO WHEELS AND AIRSCREW

technically a tank since the turret does not rotate, is equipped with a 75mm gun and is sufficiently light in weight to be transported by the detachable wing system. The Christie armored vehicle could operate with the tracks removed, so the system is technically feasible in that the armored vehicle could land at high speed. There is a power take-off at the rear of the engine with a rotating shaft rising vertically to a bevel gear that drives the main propeller shaft. The vertical shaft detaches quickly when the airframe is released. The armored vehicle can travel at nearly 100mph so landing, say at 60mph, would not be a problem. The secret to his design was the light weight of the armored vehicle, making it feasible for airborne operations.

Despite all the innovative ideas and prototypes, Christie's designs were never produced. Several foreign countries utilized parts or all of the Christie designs and patent. Christie's designs were light weight, low profile, high speed and well armed, but deficient in armor protection.

The Russian Antonov A-40 was an airborne tank design using an existing T-60 light tank. The glider would be towed aloft using

Flying 'tank' concept showing the self-propelled flying system. (*Popular Mechanics,* Vol. 58)

View of the Christie tank hull and engine installation. The bearing supports at the top of the frame are for the shaft that drives the propeller for the flying tank. Aluminum was used throughout the hull, resulting in a relatively lightweight armored vehicle. (*Popular Mechanics,* Vol. 65)

Side view of the Christie hull showing lightweight aluminum wheels with pneumatic tires. (*Modern Mechanics and Inventions*, Vol. VIII)

The front view of the hull showing the driver location in the center and front idler shaft. (*Modern Mechanics and Inventions*, Vol. VIII)

An alternative method of armored vehicle delivery to a battlefield was to attach the armored vehicle to the belly of a large aircraft, as shown here. The armored vehicle driver would match the speed of the tracks with that of the aircraft so that the vehicle could be released without pitching over. (*Popular Mechanics*, Vol. 65)

An M 1937 Christie airborne tank sold to the British. (Chamberlain and Pugh, *T.3 Christie*)

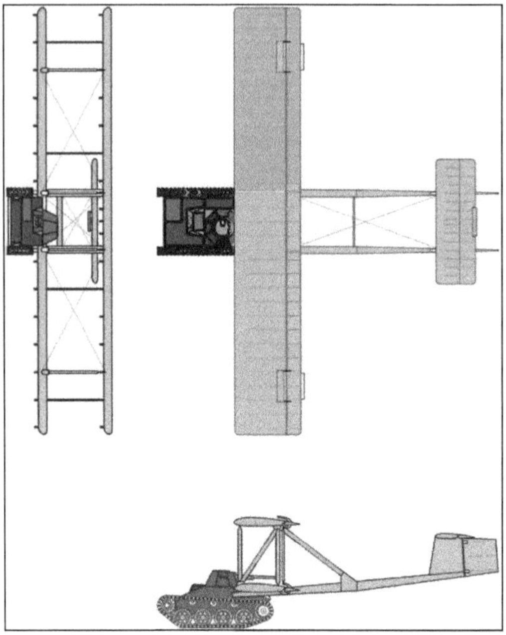

An Antonov A-40 Krylya Tanka.

a large aircraft, released over the battlefield, land, discard the glider adapter wings and proceed to the battle area. Oleg Antonov, the famed Russian aircraft designer, created a plan for a glider attachment to a light tank. The idea of attaching wings to a tank was not unique as it had previously been proposed in 1932.* The biplane was constructed of wood and fabric with an adapter for a light tank. The wingspan was approximately 59ft with a total wing area of approximately 923 sq. ft. According to Soviet authorities, there was a successful flight of the aircraft in September 1942 using a T-60 light tank, but this design was considered impractical. First of all, the tank would probably have had difficulty handling the landing speed of the glider. Many tracked vehicles were only capable of speeds up to 50mph, above which the track tended to disintegrate. It should be noted that if a tank is traveling at 50mph, the top track sections are traveling at 100mph. The inertia of the track system would probably be so high that the tank would pitch over rather than stay level with the track accelerating to the proper speed. This necessitates the pilot starting the engine and accelerating the tracks to match the landing speed. This increases the chance of throwing a track, which is more likely to occur with suspended tracks that typically sag below the road wheels. Second, it was not clear how to recover the bulky glider wings and fuselage for further usage. Third, the aerodynamic drag was probably significant and very few aircraft could act as a tug. Fourth, the T60 is a very lightly armed vehicle and probably would not have contributed significantly to the battle. Fifth, the ammunition and fuel had to be brought in separately in order to reduce the weight on the glider, which would delay the tank engaging in combat. This concept was discarded in favor of using a powered aircraft to carry the tank.

* *Popular Mechanics*, Vol. 58, Number 1, 1932.

The next stage in Russian development of the flying tank concept was securing a light tank to the fuselage of a TB-3 bomber. The tank used was the Soviet T-37, an amphibious tank based on the Carden Loyd design with modifications. Carden Loyd, a British company, had manufactured several models of small tankettes, which were purchased by a number of countries. The T-37 was manufactured by the Soviets under license from Carden Loyd with the main armament being a 7.62mm DT machine gun, with no larger guns. The tankette was hoisted under the belly of the TB-3 bomber and several tests were performed for deployment. It is not clear on the condition of the tank after a drop into water or on land. The aircraft speed was high and upon reaching the ground or water, the possibility existed of the tank tumbling and coming to rest inverted. The tracks most likely could not handle the speed when landing on ground and there was a high probability of throwing a track due to the slack in the dry pin track design. No operable system was developed from this testing.

A Tupolev TB-3. (Kolomiets, *Tanki-amfibii T-37, T-38, T-40*)

A Tupolev TB-3 and T-37 Amphibious tank. (Kolomiets, *Tanki-amfibii T-37, T-38, T-40*)

Above and below: A T-37A Amphibious tank under the TB-3. (*T37-A Soviet Amphibious Tank – Case Report*)

The ME 323 Gigant was used by the Germans to transport armored vehicles, as seen above. (http://www.ww2incolor.com)

The ME 323 Gigant was originally designed by the Germans as an assault glider to deliver armored vehicles to England (Operation Sea Lion). Glider assaults in Belgium and Crete proved successful, giving impetus to the development of a large assault glider. As a result of British success in the Battle of Britain, which denied the Germans air superiority, Sea Lion was cancelled, but the development of the large assault glider continued for possible use in the invasion of the Soviet Union (Operation Barbarossa). The requirement for the glider was that it be able to carry an armored vehicle the size of a Panzerkampfwagen IV. Messerschmidt won the competition to develop the glider resulting in the ME 321. One problem with the glider was the difficulty experienced by the tug aircraft towing such a large load. Experiments performed using two aircraft proved dangerous. The ME 321 was used in the invasion of Russia, but due to pilot input it was decided to manufacture a motorized version, the ME 323 Gigant. The wing was redesigned to allow six engines, and fixed wheels were added under the fuselage. The three engines on one wing rotated in the opposite direction to those on the other wing to cancel out engine torque effects on the flight characteristics of the aircraft.

The aircraft had wings made of plywood and fabric while the fuselage was metal tubing covered with fabric. The crew comprised two pilots, two flight engineers and a radio operator. The maximum payload was approximately 24,000lb using rocket-assisted take-off units. The cargo compartment was 36ft long, 10ft wide and 11ft high. The top speed was 136mph. Defensive armament was several machine guns mounted on the top of the fuselage behind the wing. The ME 323 was used in the Tunisian Campaign to supply the Afrika Korps, since Allied warships were taking a heavy toll on German shipping. The range of the ME 323 was approximately 700 miles. The aircraft was under-powered and an easy target for Allied fighters because of its size and slow speed. The aircraft was used extensively through the remainder of the war as a vehicle and troop transport, making it one of the more successful of the tank-carrying aircraft.

In 1942, the Japanese developed a large glider with a load-carrying capacity of 16,755lb, the Kokusai Ku-7. It could carry a light tank. A few aircraft, such as the Nakajima Ki-49 and the Mitsubishi Ki-67, could act as a tug. These aircraft were needed for bombing missions,

A Kokusai Ku-7 Glider. (https://commons.wikimedia.org/wiki/Commons)

so engines were fitted to the glider. Despite an order for 300 aircraft, only 9 were ever delivered. The glider had a crew of two and could carry thirty-two troops, a tank or an artillery piece plus its tractor. Its length was 64ft, wing span 114ft, and when empty weighed 10,000lb. The maximum towing speed was 125mph. The Ku 7 was never used in combat.

The British Army became interested in airborne operations in 1940 as a result of German success with airborne assaults and also the influence of Winston Churchill. It was decided that gliders should become the major airborne means of transporting troops and equipment to the battlefield. The Air Ministry specified four types of gliders to be developed, the largest of which was to carry a light tank. General Aircraft Ltd (GAL) was chosen to develop a large glider that could carry a light tank. In 1941 the design of the GAL 49 glider was completed and named the Hamilcar after Hamilcar Barca, a Carthaginian general. The first flight on 27 March 1942 using a Handley Page Halifax bomber as the tow aircraft was a success.

The Hamilcar, the largest glider made by the British, had a wingspan of 110ft, length of 68ft, a height of 20ft and weighed 18,400lb empty. The load capacity was 17,600lb. The glider could be disassembled into sections that were easily transported by truck. Only the largest, most

A British General Aircraft Ltd (GAL) Hamilcar glider landing with full flaps at approximately 54mph. (Wikimedia Commons)

powerful, four-engine bomber could act as a tug for this glider. The glider was of wood construction with aluminum sections in critical areas. The skin was fabric. The cargo area was approximately 33ft by 8ft by 7ft. Exit from the cargo area was the nose of the aircraft which opened from one side like a clam shell. The doctrine of the British Airborne Force at the time was to release the glider at low altitude, descend steeply to avoid enemy fire, land at low speed for better control on unimproved surfaces. Large flaps were required to provide braking during a steep descent and slow landing speed. Landing approach speed was 100mph with a stall speed of 64mph without flaps and 54mph with flaps. The Hamilcar was used in Operation Overlord and Operation Market Garden for carrying Tetrarch light tanks and in Operation Varsity for carrying Locust light tanks. Of all the efforts of other nations utilizing airborne tanks, this British method of delivering a tank to the battlefield was the most successful during the course of the Second World War.

Several countries experimented with airborne-tank delivery systems. They utilized existing light tanks which were adapted to available air frames. The US Army in concert with the British Army developed the first tank designed specifically for airborne operations, the M22 Locust.

A Tetrarch light tank exiting a Hamilcar glider. (https://ww2db.com)

Chapter 2

The US Airborne Tank

At the beginning of the Second World War in Europe, airborne troop operations pioneered by the Germans were making a significant impact on military doctrine. Their success in spearheading operations in the Netherlands, Norway and Greece did not go unnoticed by the British. In early 1941, the British wanted to develop a tank designed for airborne operations to be delivered by air. The British Air Commission in Washington DC first made overtures to the American Ordnance Department for the design of an airborne tank. Britain lacked the industrial capacity to produce such a tank. There were material shortages because of German attacks on seaborne convoys that limited imports as well as other higher priority projects utilizing resources. The disaster at Dunkirk resulted in a substantial loss of vehicles and other fighting equipment and this needed to be replaced. The British were the only ally in Europe opposing the Germans. They needed to upgrade their present tank (Tetrarch) which was not designed for airborne operations but was expected to be used for such a role if no other tanks became available. They hoped America would provide such an upgrade under the Lend Lease Act of 1941.

Initial specifications suggested that the tank weigh 9 to 10 tons, have a 37mm main gun and a 0.30 cal. Browning machine gun in the turret, have a maximum speed of 40mph and a 200-mile range, as well as frontal armor of approximately 50mm, side armor of about 30mm and a crew of three (driver, gunner and commander loader). The Ordnance Department was not enthusiastic about the proposal. The United States was not in the war as yet, and current production capacity was near its limits. The United States had no way to deliver the tank and the proposed glider that would deliver the tank had not yet been built by the British. The British already had a light tank with similar specifications, the Tetrarch Mk VII, but it was considered inadequate for supporting lightly armed airborne units that typically spearheaded an invasion, and the Tetrarch was not designed as an airborne tank.

It was the success of German airborne operations that finally got this joint project rolling. German airborne units, when deployed, quickly reached their objective and contributed to the overall effectiveness of their campaigns. In May 1940, German airborne troops (Fallschirmjager) captured a substantial fortification in Belgium (Fort Eben Emael) defended by over 1,000 Belgian troops. During the Netherlands invasion, the German 7th Air Division captured bridges at Moerdijk and Dordrecht, allowing German armor to continue the Blitzkrieg. This impressed the United States and Britain. In early 1941, the Ordnance Department had a meeting with the members of the Armored Force, Army Air Corps, General Staff and with British representatives to discuss the development of an airborne tank and a delivery system. The British were influential as to the design requirements, although the United States preferred a powered aircraft to deliver the tank rather than a glider. It was decided to proceed with the development of an American airborne light tank.

Engineering began with the vehicle weight objective of 7.5 tons. The dimensions were such that the vehicle should fit in a Hamilcar glider. Three contractors were invited to submit proposals for the new airborne tank T-9: General Motors Pontiac Division, Marmon-Herrington and Walter Christie. The Walter Christie design did not meet specifications after two proposals were submitted and was no longer considered. Walter Christie was a talented designer but was difficult to work with. His idea of what the US Army tank should be differed from what the Ordnance Department wanted, resulting in disagreements and finally, dismissal from the competition. The Armored Tank Corporation, which had purchased technology from Walter Christie, was not asked to submit a proposal. The General Motors design incorporating two engines was considered too expensive. The winner was Marmon-Herrington. Marmon had designed tanks in the past and had sold them to foreign countries and the US Army, an example being the T14 tank that was utilized in Alaska.

In the early 1930s, the Marmon-Herrington Company also provided aircraft refueling trucks, reconnaissance cars, scout cars and other vehicles to the US military and other foreign countries. The Marmon-Herrington armored car was used by the British in North Africa.

The first prototype of the new airborne tank, designated Light Tank T-9 Airborne, was delivered in late 1941. It was a low-profile tank

A Tetrarch Mk VII light tank – weight 16,800lb, 40mm main gun, 7.92mm machine gun, crew of three. (https://commons.wikimedia.org/wiki/Commons)

Marmon-Herrington T14 tanks in Alaska. (Library of Congress)

An early wood mock-up of the T-9 tank. (Marmon-Herrington Company)

with a powered turret and gyro-stabilized 37mm gun like that of the M5 light tank. This gyro stabilizing system was essentially a gun-tube leveler, which was very advanced for its day. There were three 0.30 cal. machine guns, one in the turret and two on the right side of the front glacis plate. The gun leveler, powered turret and two of the machine guns were later eliminated to save weight. The suspension was two road-wheel assemblies on each side of the tank with a total of four road wheels on each side with volute springs. The Christie suspension design was not incorporated. The power unit was a six-cylinder opposed, air cooled, Lycoming aircraft engine (O-435-T) to save weight. The engine developed 162HP at 2,800RPM. The front armor thickness at the glacis plate was approximately 12.5mm, but because of the slope the equivalent was roughly 25mm. The three-man crew comprised a driver, a gunner and a commander/loader. Because of the low tank profile, the driver essentially had to sit on the floor of the hull, next to the rotating propeller shaft.

The T-9 was designed to be carried by a C-54 cargo plane. This required that the turret be removed and placed in the plane. Four lifting lugs were provided to hoist the hull under the belly of the plane. This method of delivery was problematic. The C-54 could only land on prepared runways. Runways near the battlefield were typically badly damaged, precluding usage by this type of aircraft. After all, the purpose of the airborne tank was to deploy behind enemy lines with the airborne force. The Hamilcar was a better option since the glider could land in a field behind enemy lines.

In February 1941, the Ordnance Department met with the G-4 of the Armored Force and with Army Air Corps to consider the development of an airborne tank and a means to deliver it to the battlefield. The British wanted the development of an airborne light tank that would work with their top-secret program, which was developing a large glider to deliver such a tank (the Hamilcar). The British initially recommended a maximum weight of 7.5 tons, a length of 138in, a width of 84in and a height of 66in. The main firepower was proposed to be a 37mm or 57mm gun. In addition, several machine guns were recommended. A powered turret traversing mechanism and a crew of two or three was also proposed.

Specifications for the new light tank were developed in August 1941, and the purchase of a prototype was approved. The vehicle was low in profile, had sloped armor, a 37mm main gun and a coaxial 0.30 caliber machine gun. The hull was welded, which was much better than the riveted designs, which were hazardous when a projectile knocked off the top of the rivets, sending the rivet remains flying around the fighting compartment, injuring the occupants. There were two bow-mounted 0.30 caliber machine guns and a maximum armor thickness of 1in. The tracks were dry pin design, 11in wide and 3in long from pin to pin (pitch). The tracks were T78 Carden-Loyd design, made of malleable iron. The Carden-Loyd Company had been manufacturing tracked vehicles and tankettes prior to the beginning of the Second World War. The track tension was fairly low to reduce wear in the dry pins. If the track was drawn very tight, it would wear oval-shaped holes in the track units, which then allowed more dirt to enter and accelerate the wear.

The first prototype had problems with the suspension. The road-wheel assemblies were easily deflected and knocked out of alignment during testing. Consequently, adjustable rods were added to further support the alignment of the road-wheel assemblies in a manner similar to that of a wheeled vehicle. The maximum weight was now agreed to be 15,800lb, near the maximum load of the new Hamilcar glider. The weight of a Tetrarch was 16,800lb. After several changes, including lightening the turret, adding sloped armor to deflect projectiles, removing bow machine guns and the gyro stabilizer for the 37mm main gun, two new prototypes were ordered in January 1942, designated T-9E1 and later designated M22 Locust. The prototypes were delivered to Aberdeen

A T-9 showing bow machine gun and pistol port in the turret. (Marmon-Herrington Company)

A modified T-9 with beam supports to strengthen road-wheel supports. Hoist clevises were added for transport under the fuselage of an aircraft. (General Motors Proving Grounds)

Top view of the asymmetrical turret in the early T-9 design. (General Motors Proving Grounds)

A T-9E1 with early vintage driver's hatch. (Roberts Collection)

Proving Grounds in Maryland for testing. Apparently, the British were impressed with what they observed, and 1,900 tanks were ordered despite the fact that testing had not been completed. Delivery was to begin in November 1942, but production problems delayed the delivery start to April 1943. (It is interesting to note that other projects started production before testing was completed because of the urgency of getting the weapon into the field. The development of the B-29 Bomber is an example of once a plane was finished it had to be sent to another plant for modifications.) Details of the characteristics of the M22 Locust tank are discussed in the following pages.

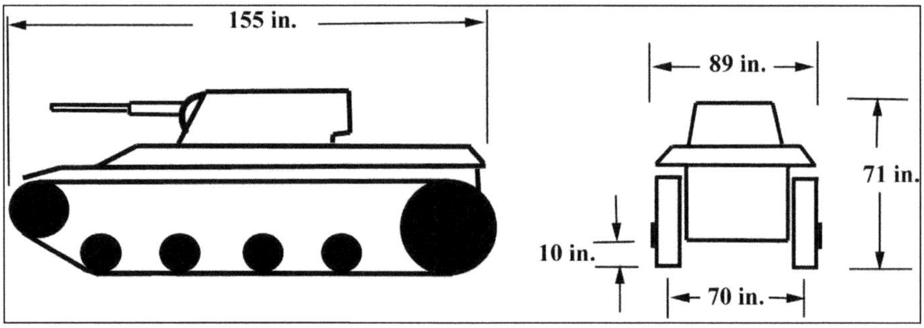

The generic dimension of the M22 light tank. (Roberts Collection)

Above and opposite: A selection of images of the final design of the T-9E1 which was later designated M22. Its weight was 16,400lb, top speed 40mph on improved roads and 30mph on cross-country routes. (TM 9-724, *Light Tank T-9E1*)

U.S.A. 3067123

The front and rear view of the M22 light tank. (TM 9-724, *Light Tank T-9E1*)

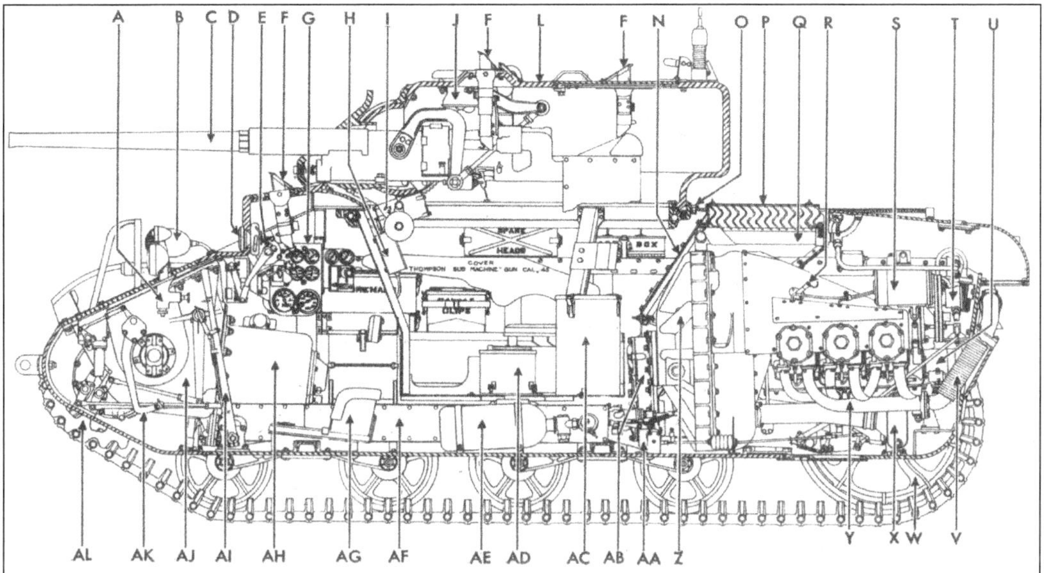

A diagram of major components of the M22 light tank. (TM 9-724, *Light Tank T-9E1*)

Technical Specifications for the M22

Armor Dimensions

Front glacis plate	½in
Front curved plate	1in
Vertical sides	½in
Sloped sides	⅜in
Top plate	⅜in
Rear	½in
Bottom plate	½in
Turret all sides	1in

Turret

Arc of rotation	360 degrees
Rotation	manual crank

Periscopes

Driver M6 Scope
Commander M6 scope
Gunner M8 Sighting Scope

Dimensions and Capacity

Weight without equipment, fuel, crew	14,600lb
Weight with equipment, fuel and crew	16,400lb
Width	89in
Length	155in
Height	71in
Tread width (center to center of track)	70.25in
Ground clearance	10in
Track contact with ground	2,306.25in
Ground pressure (4in deflection)	5.97psi

Performance

Turning radius	20ft
Maximum grade with standard track	26 degrees
Maximum possible grade (perfect traction)	45 degrees
Maximum tilt	45 degrees
Maximum trench-crossing distance	65in
Fording depth	38in
Maximum vertical obstacle	12⅜in
Height of towing shakes above grade	235/16in
Maximum speed prepared road	40mph
Speed cross country	30mph
Mileage	2.5mpg in 3rd gear
Cruising range	135 miles

Communication Equipment

Radio	SCR-510

Armament

1 gun, 37mm on M6 mount
1 machine gun, cal. 0.30
1 Thompson submachine gun, cal. 45

Ammunition Stored

37mm	50 rounds
Cal. 0.30	2,500 rounds

Above: The top view of the T-9E1 showing the final, more symmetrical turret design. (TM 9-724, *Light Tank T-9E1*)

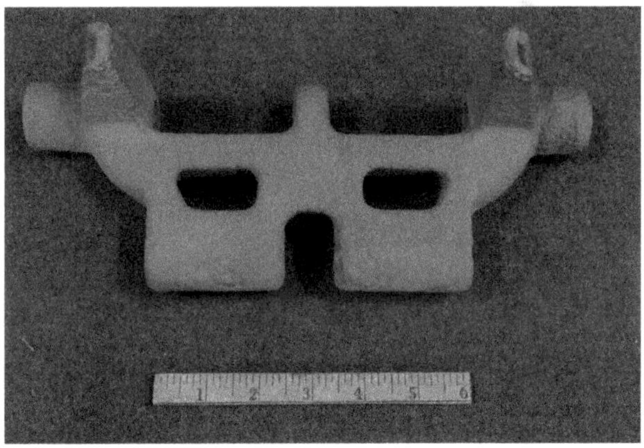

Right: A T78 Carden-Loyd track used on the T-9E1. This is the road-wheel side of the track. (Roberts Collection)

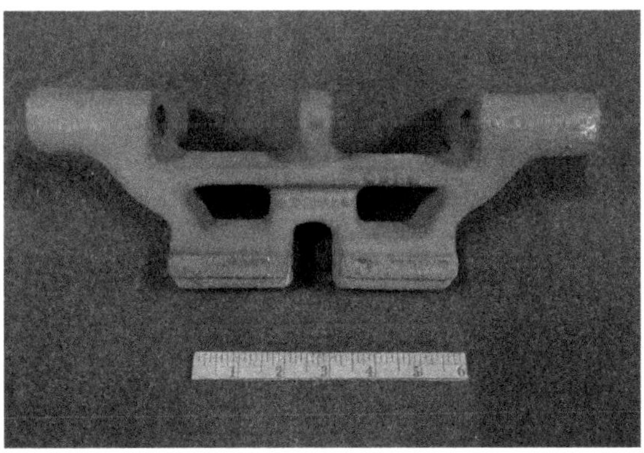

A Carden-Loyd track viewed from the ground side. There are small grousers on each end of the track that accept the track pin. The track link is of minimum weight in order to comply with the vehicle weight limitation of 8 tons. (Roberts Collection)

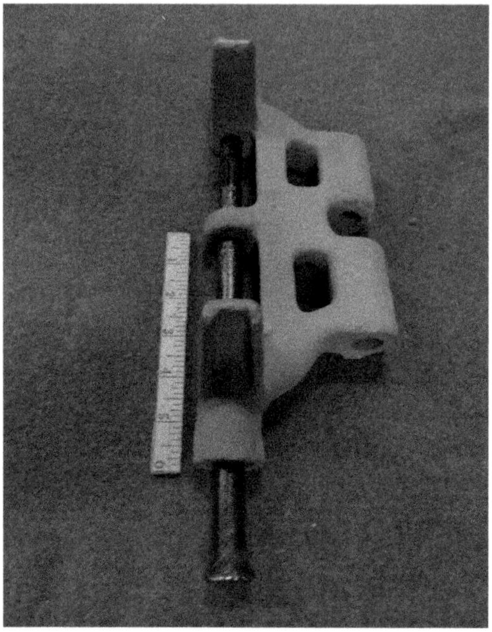

Left: The track link with track pin. The hole that accepts the track pin is approximately 0.65in. If the track is adjusted with excessive tension (virtually no sag in the track), severe wear results and the track becomes loose. (Roberts Collection)

Below: A T16 track block for the M5A1 Stuart Tank. This track had rubber bushings for the pins that would hardly wear compared with the Carden-Loyd design. (Roberts Collection)

The track at the rear idler wheel. (Roberts Collection)

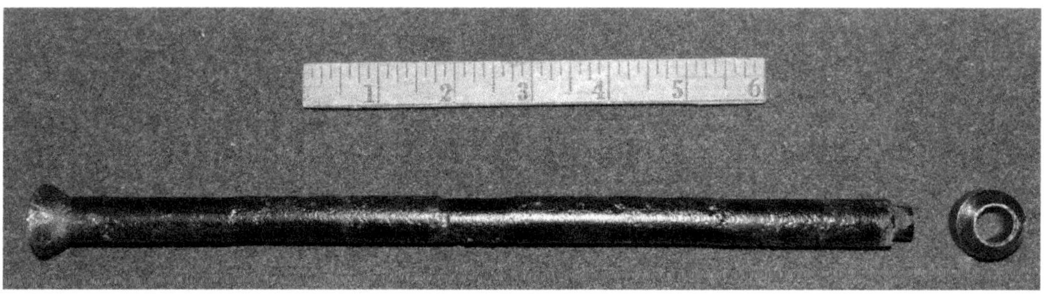

A track pin and retainer from M22, serial number 110. The shaft shows typical wear on a track pin removed from the vehicle. A special tool is used to stake the retainer onto the pin as shown on the following page. To remove a pin, another special tool is placed at the staked end and a hammer is used to drive out the pin. (Roberts Collection)

The staking operation to secure a track pin. The pin is placed in the track and the retainer is inserted over the small shoulder at the end of a pin. The staking tool is then driven into the retainer, securing the pin. To remove the pin another tool is placed at the center of the pin and a hammer drives out the pin. (Roberts Collection)

The staked end of the pin showing the stake mark. To remove the pin a centering tool is driven into the center of the pin which shears off the old retainer. In the photograph above right the other end of the pin shows the forged outer end. The forged end of the pin is always on the outside and the staked end is always on the inside. (Roberts Collection)

The unsupported road-wheel assemblies were not sufficiently robust to handle normal tank terrain operations. (Marmon-Herrington Company)

I-beams were used to support the assemblies on an early prototype shown previously, but efforts to reduce the vehicle weight resulted in the adjustable support-brace configuration seen here. (Roberts Collection)

The road-wheel (bogie) assembly is aligned by adjusting the nut and fitting at the end of the support bar. A brace is placed near the road wheels to aid in the adjustment. Poor alignment results in road-wheel rubber tire wear and the possibility of throwing a track. (TM 9-724, *Light Tank T-9E1*)

Above left: The drive sprocket for the T-9 prototype. (Marmon-Herrington Company)

Above right: The drive sprocket was deemed too heavy, and subsequent early production models had a much thinner stamped sprocket as seen here. This was found to be too thin so later models had double the thickness. (Roberts Collection)

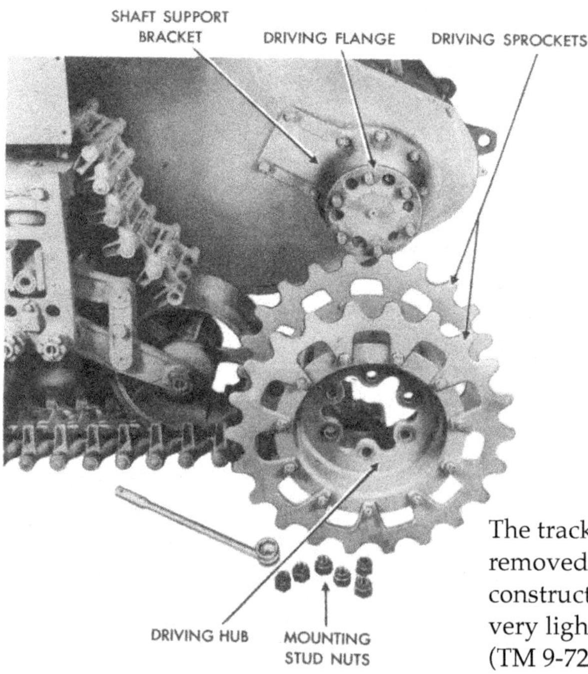

The track drive sprocket being removed. The sprocket is constructed of stampings and is very light for a sprocket design. (TM 9-724, *Light Tank T-9E1*)

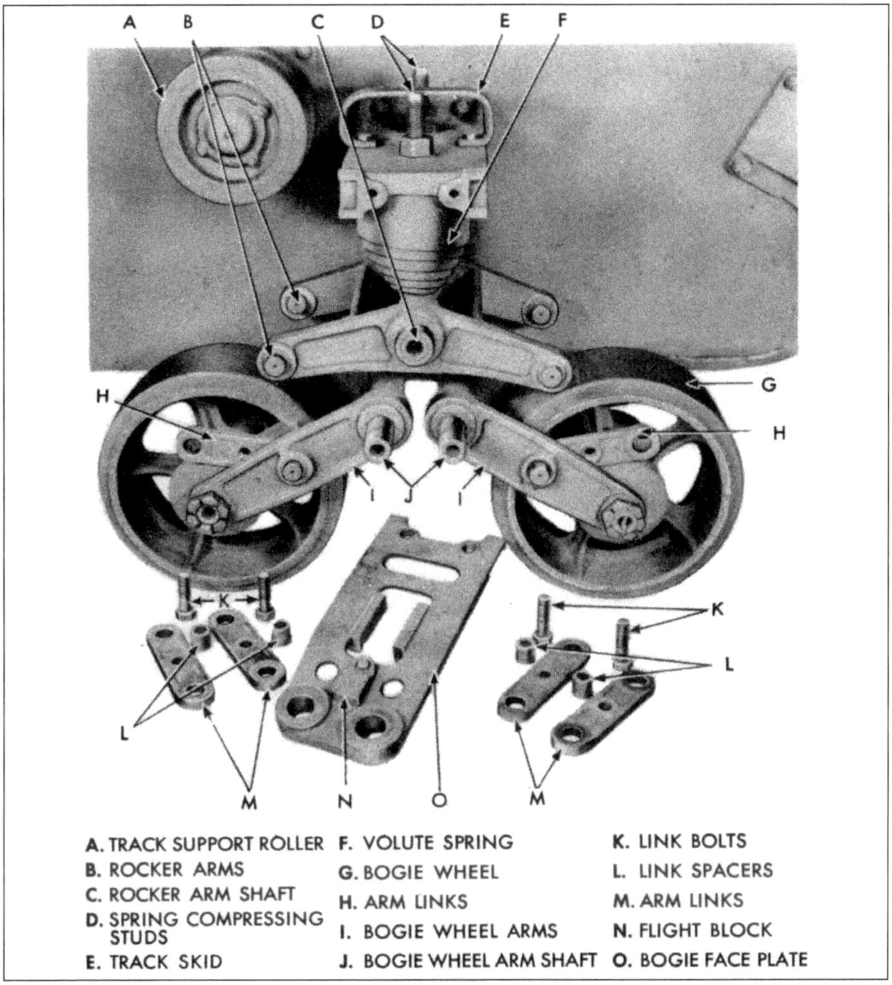

Above and right: There are two road-wheel assemblies on each side using volute springs. Two track support wheels were on each side to keep the track off the support frames. Volute springs absorb the irregularities in the terrain but not as effectively as the Christie suspension. (Roberts Collection)

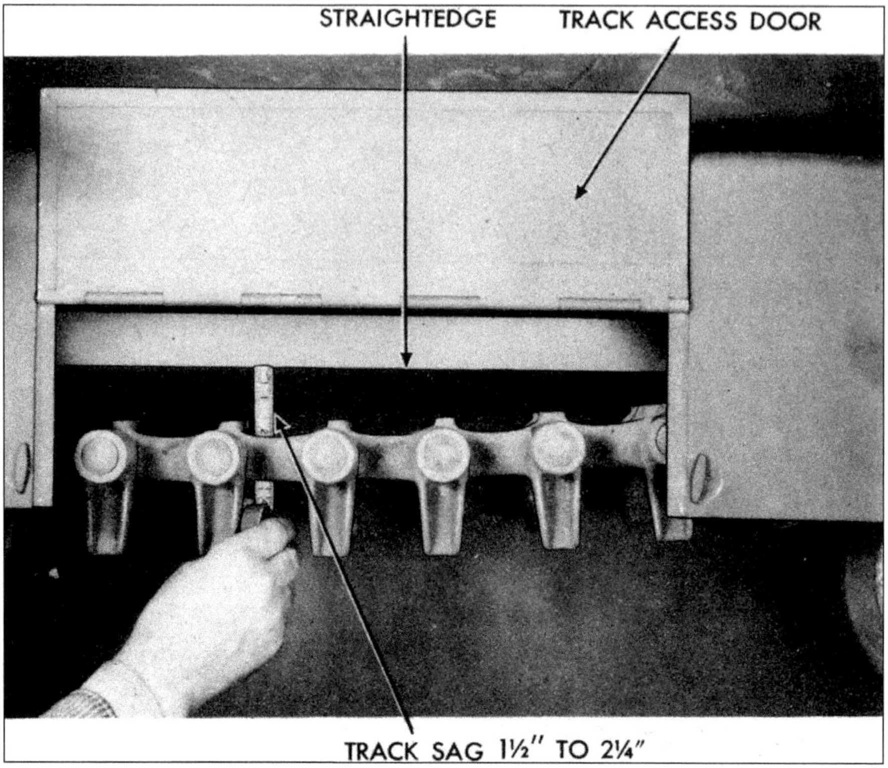

The proper track adjustment is made between the two support rollers. This slack track adjustment helps reduce wear but can result in throwing a track when traveling downhill and suddenly turning right or left. (TM 9-724, *Light Tank T-9E1*)

The rear idler wheel adjustments. To tension the track, one must release the large nut at the end of the idler axle shaft (left arrow in photograph) and then turn the small nut (right arrow) slightly to the right clockwise for tensioning. (Roberts Collection)

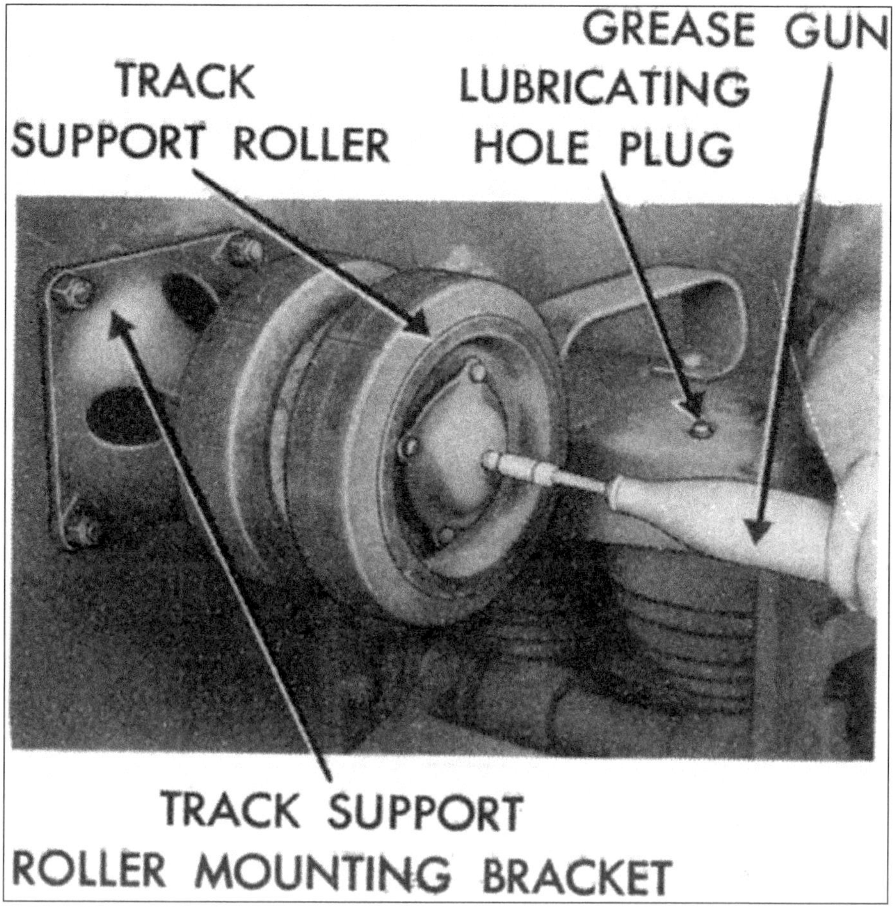

Lubricating the track support wheel. (TM 9-724, *Light Tank T-9E1*)

A track support roller manufactured by Firestone Tire and Rubber Company. There are two on each side. (Roberts Collection)

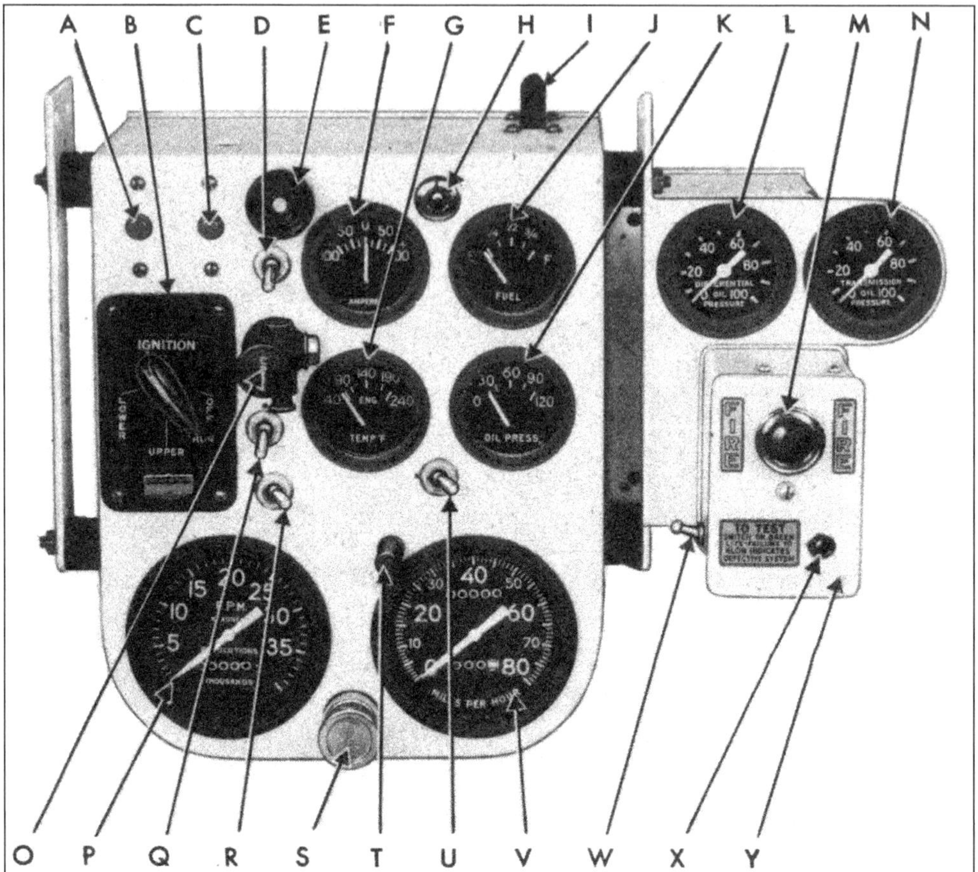

A. CIRCUIT BREAKER RESET BUTTON (HEAD LIGHT)
B. IGNITION SWITCH
C. CIRCUIT BREAKER RESET BUTTON (INSTRUMENTS)
D. BLACKOUT LIGHT SWITCH
E. SIREN BUTTON
F. AMMETER
G. ENGINE OIL TEMPERATURE GAGE
H. LOW OIL PRESSURE SIGNAL LIGHT (RED)
I. MASTER SWITCH
J. FUEL GAGE
K. ENGINE OIL PRESSURE GAGE
L. DIFFERENTIAL OIL PRESSURE GAGE
M. FIRE DETECTOR SIGNAL LIGHT (RED)
N. TRANSMISSION OIL PRESSURE GAGE
O. MASTER LIGHT SWITCH
P. TACHOMETER
Q. DETENT SWITCH
R. STARTER SWITCH
S. PRIMER
T. SPEEDOMETER RESET BUTTON
U. INSTRUMENT PANEL LIGHT SWITCH
V. SPEEDOMETER
W. FIRE DETECTOR CHECK LIGHT SWITCH
X. FIRE DETECTOR CHECK LIGHT
Y. FIRE DETECTOR CONTROL BOX

The control panel for M22 driver. (TM 9-724, *Light Tank T-9E1*)

The diagram to the left shows the panel of switches and gauges used to operate the tank. This panel is located to the right of the driver. The ignition switch (B) is of interest. It has four positions: Off, Run, Lower and Upper. Off turns off the engine; the Run position is used for normal operation; the Lower position connects only the lower set of spark plugs while the Upper connects only the upper set of spark plugs. Since the engine is of aircraft design, it has dual ignition. (The usage of the Lycoming aircraft engine in this vehicle was probably to save weight.)

While running, the driver selects either Upper or Lower to check the ignition system. If selecting Lower and the RPM drops slightly, that is normal. If the engine runs rough, there is an ignition problem at the lower plugs which should be corrected. The same procedure is applied for the upper set of plugs. Starting was always a tricky task. Prime the engine too much, and a fire could develop from backfiring; prime too little, and the engine would not start. Note the fire detection signal light at position (M).

Shown in the top photo on the next page is the escape hatch, which is not very useful. The opening is small, cramped and only 10in, at most, above the ground.

The driver position with seat at lower left. (TM 9-724, *Light Tank T-9E1*)

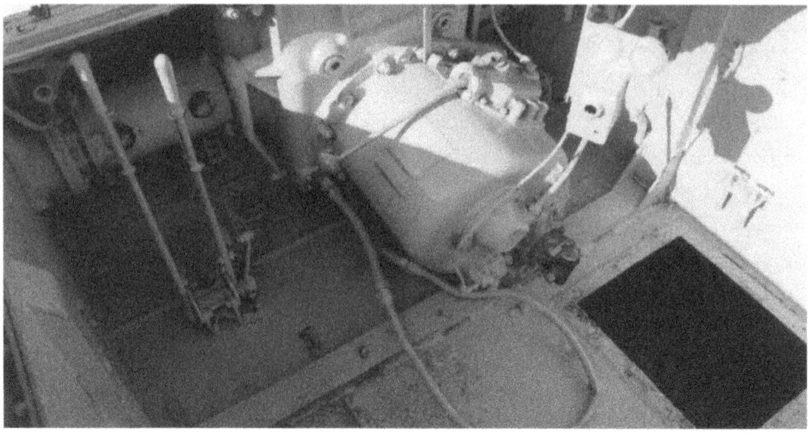

The escape hatch opening is seen lower right. (Roberts Collection)

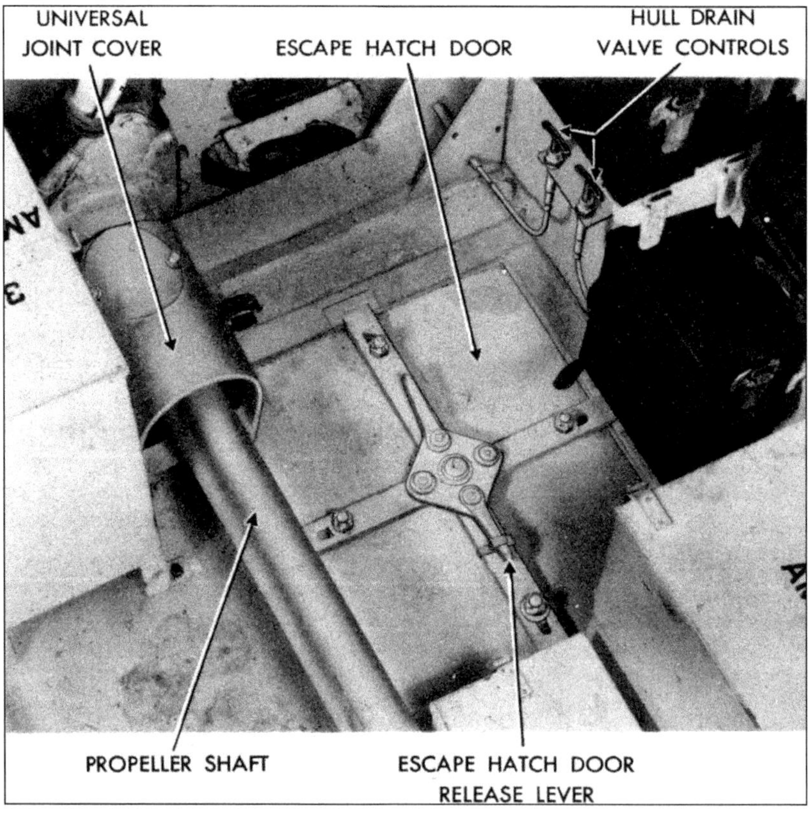

The escape hatch to the right of the transmission is secured. (TM 9-724, *Light Tank T-9E1*)

The M22 turret being removed. The turret was designed to be easily removed for loading into a C-54 cargo plane. (TM 9-724, *Light Tank T-9E1*)

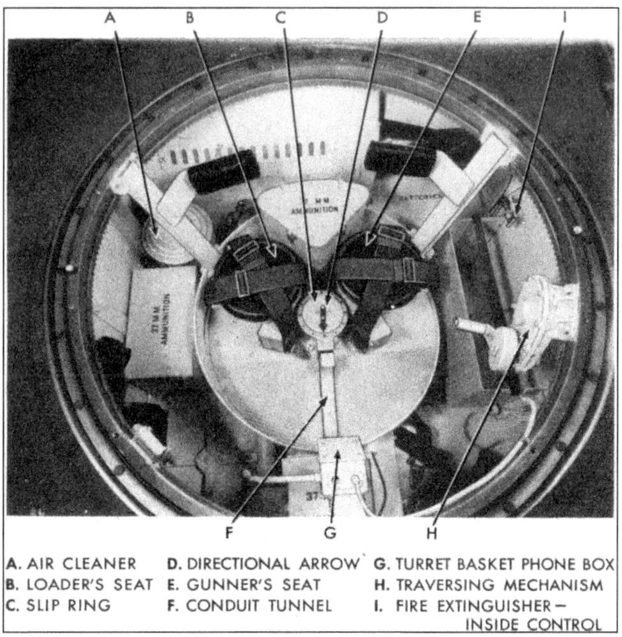

The interior of the fighting compartment. The two seats (B and E) are supported by a turret basket that rotates with the turret. The traversing mechanism is a manual crank to save weight over the powered systems normally found in American tanks of the Second World War. (TM 9-724, *Light Tank T-9E1*)

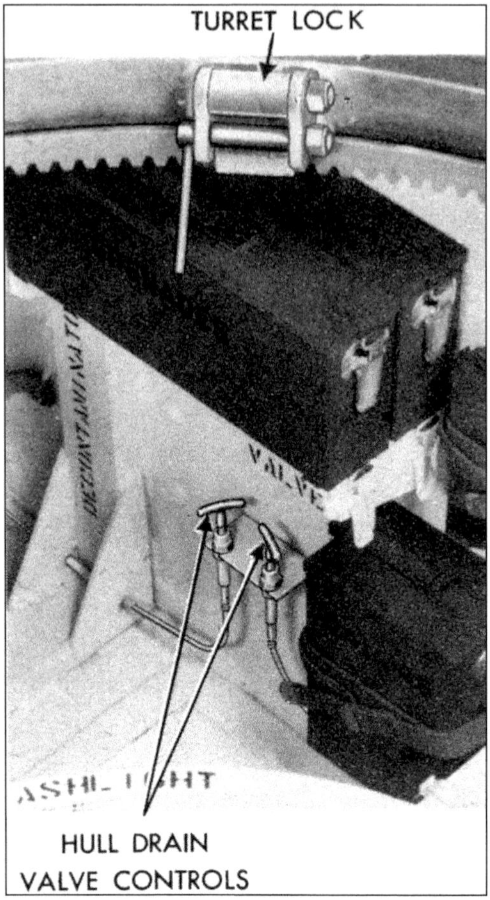

The right-hand side of the interior of the turret showing the turret traversing lock. The small valve handles allow draining of water from the hull. (TM 9-724, *Light Tank T-9E1*)

The hand crank for lifting the driver's hatch just to the right of the driver's seat. The hatch could not be raised enough to allow the driver to escape. The driver had to crawl up to the turret and out of the turret hatch to escape. (TM 9-724, *Light Tank T-9E1*)

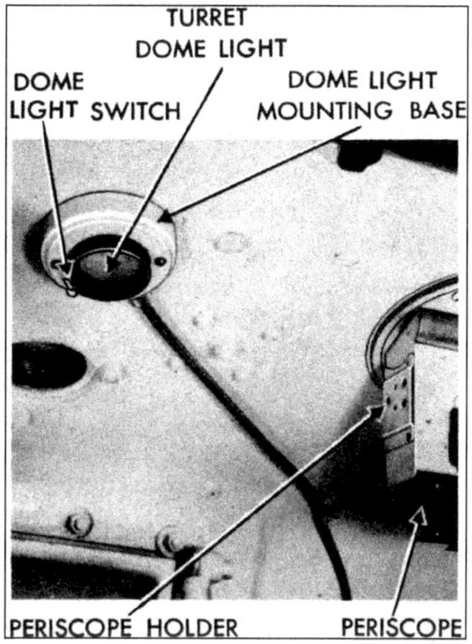

Right: The inside of the turret showing the light toward the front and the M6 periscope slot to the right. (TM 9-724, *Light Tank T-9E1*)

Below: The compass to the right of the main gun mount in the turret. A compass inside a tank had to be very large to detect the magnetic field through the steel armor. (TM 9-724, *Light Tank T-9E1*)

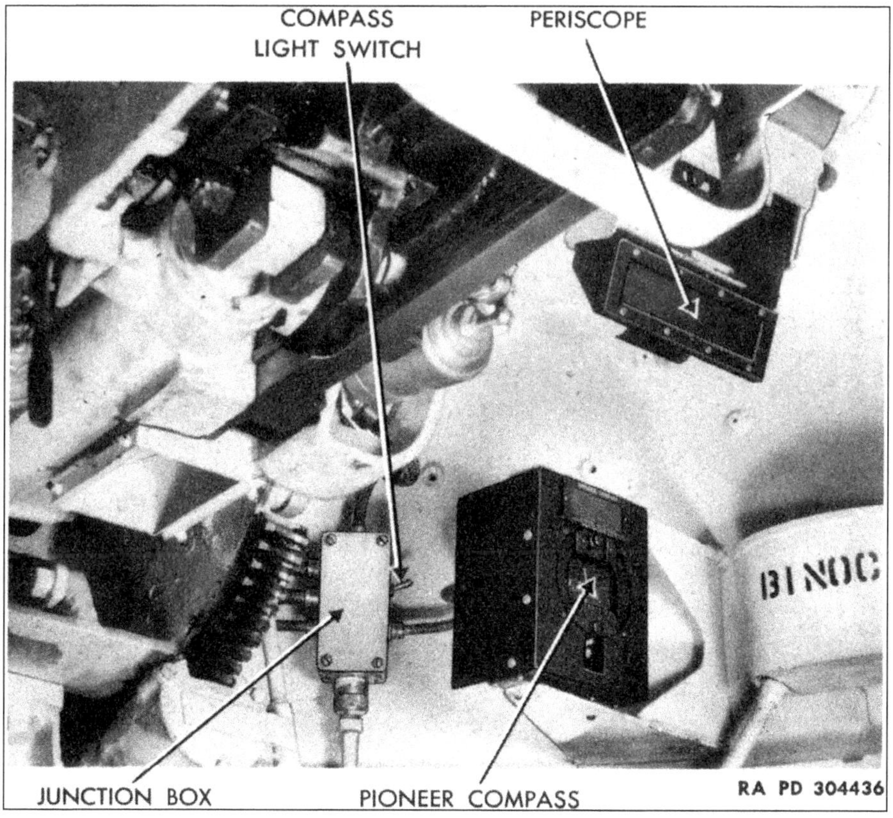

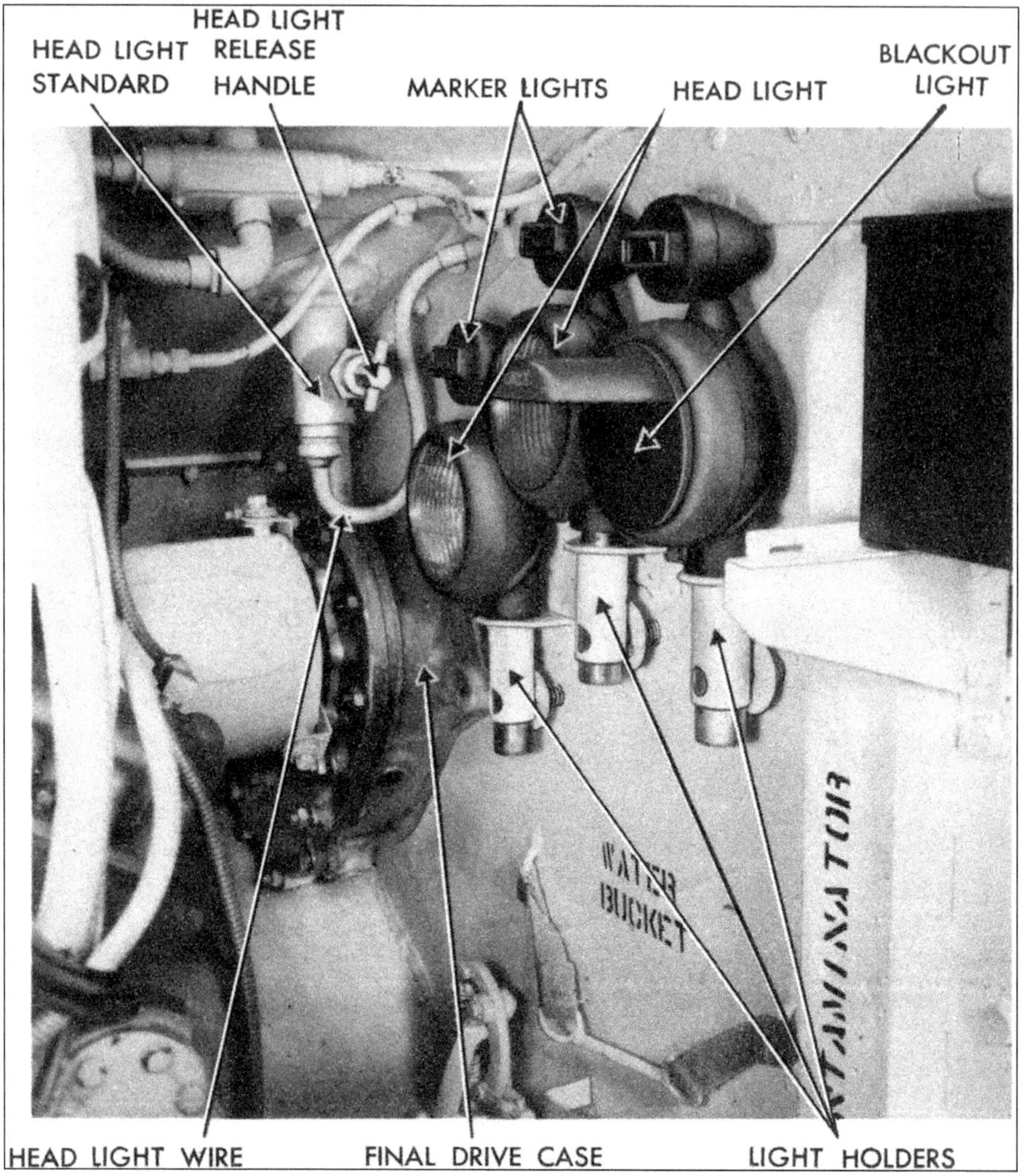

Above: The right front of the hull showing headlight stowage during battle. (TM 9-724, *Light Tank T-9E1*)

Opposite: A close-up of the hand-crank traversing mechanism with a gear reduction gear box. (TM 9-724, *Light Tank T-9E1*)

TRAVERSING
MECHANISM
CAL..30 GUN
SWITCHES
CAL..30 GUN
SWITCH WIRE
CAL. .30
AMMUNITION
PORTABLE FIRE EXTINGUISHER
DRIVER'S SEAT BACK

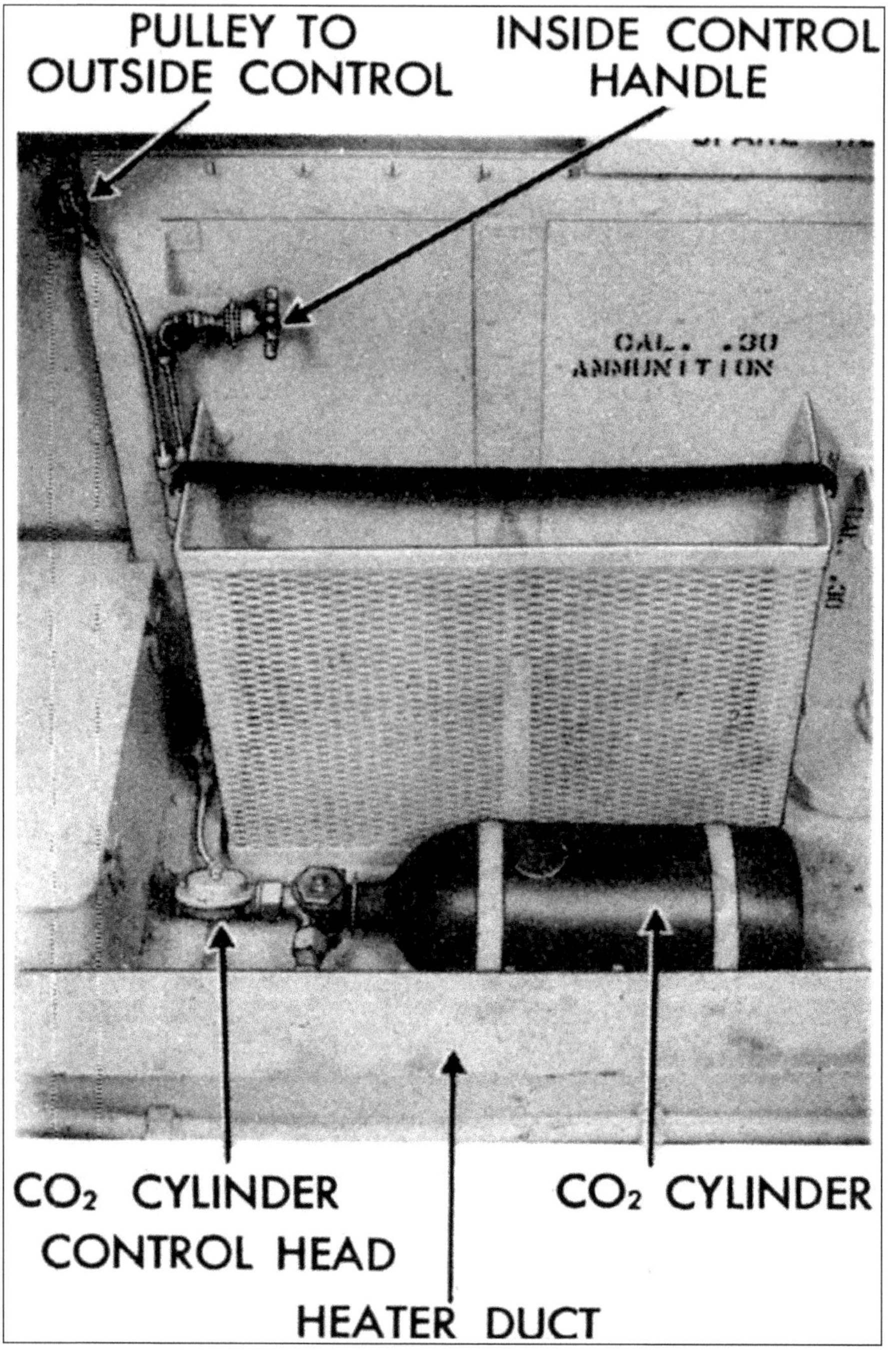

The inside view of fire-suppression system with carbon dioxide cylinder and inside control valve. (TM 9-724, *Light Tank T-9E1*)

Above: The fire-suppression system release handle outside the left side of the vehicle near the rear of the turret. (TM 9-724, *Light Tank T-9E1*)

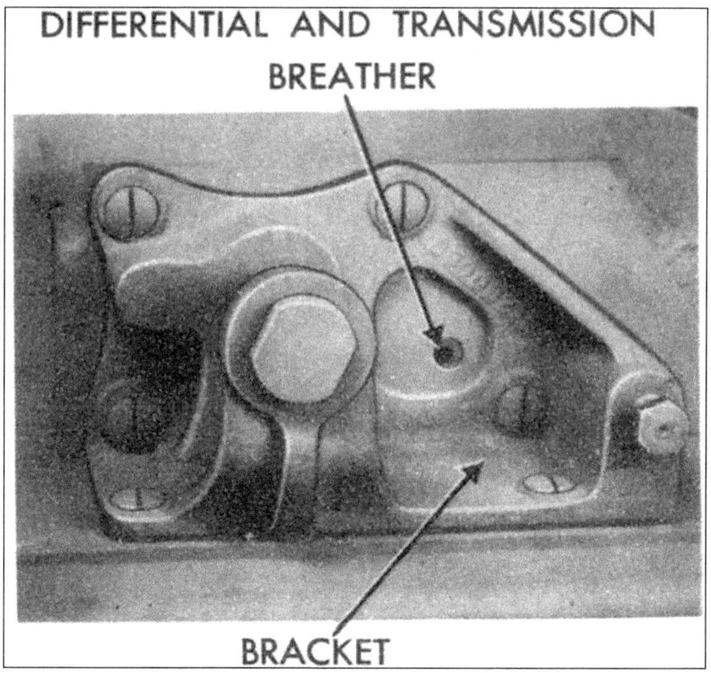

Right: The air breather from the final drive unit near a fitting used to hoist the vehicle under an aircraft. (TM 9-724, *Light Tank T-9E1*)

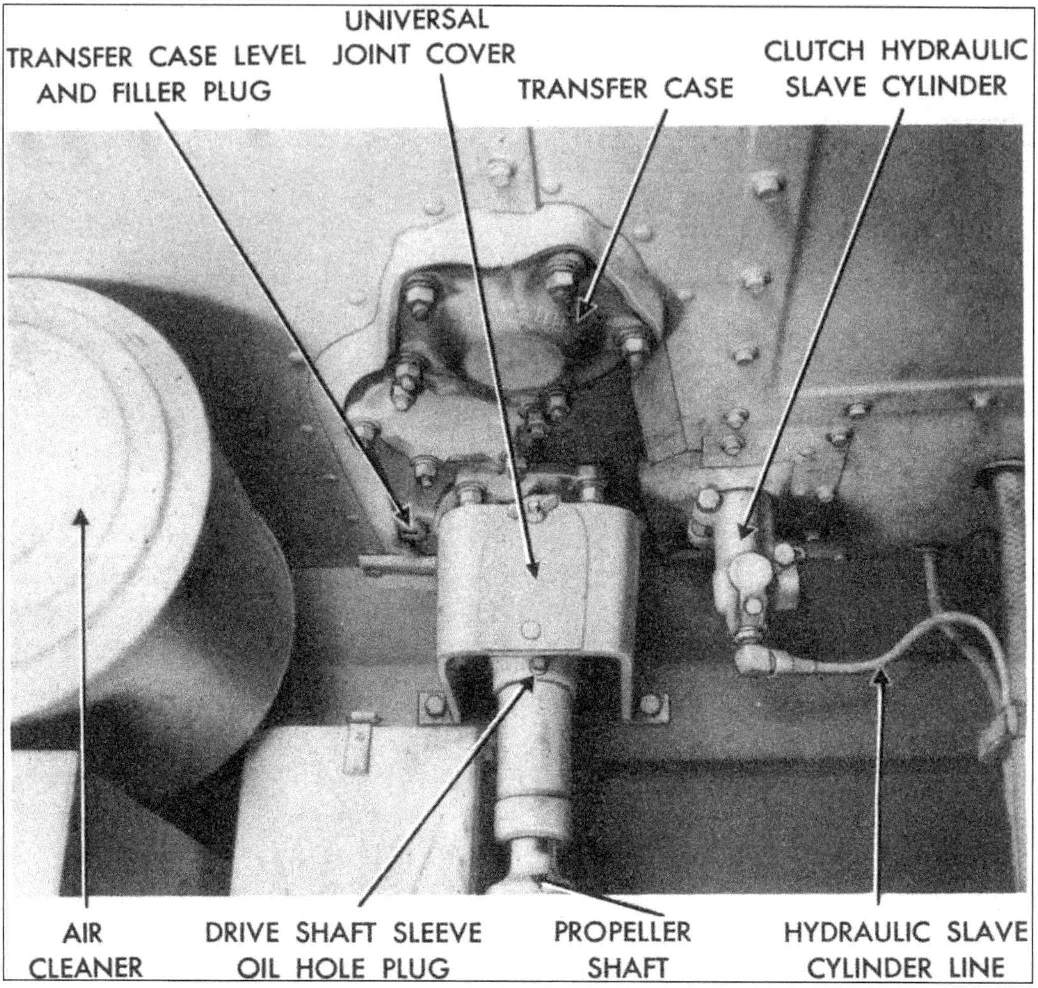

The bulkhead between the fighting compartment and the engine compartment. The clutch assembly is behind the bulkhead. The air cleaner, which is an oil bath type, is seen to the left. (TM 9-724, *Light Tank T-9E1*)

Opposite above: The engine compartment and fuel tank compartment. This allows access to ignition system components and the distributor. Access to the cartridge oil filter housing is at the right side of the compartment (left-hand side of the photograph). The gasoline fuel tank access door is at the left rear (right-hand side of the photograph) of the vehicle. (TM 9-724, *Light Tank T-9E1*)

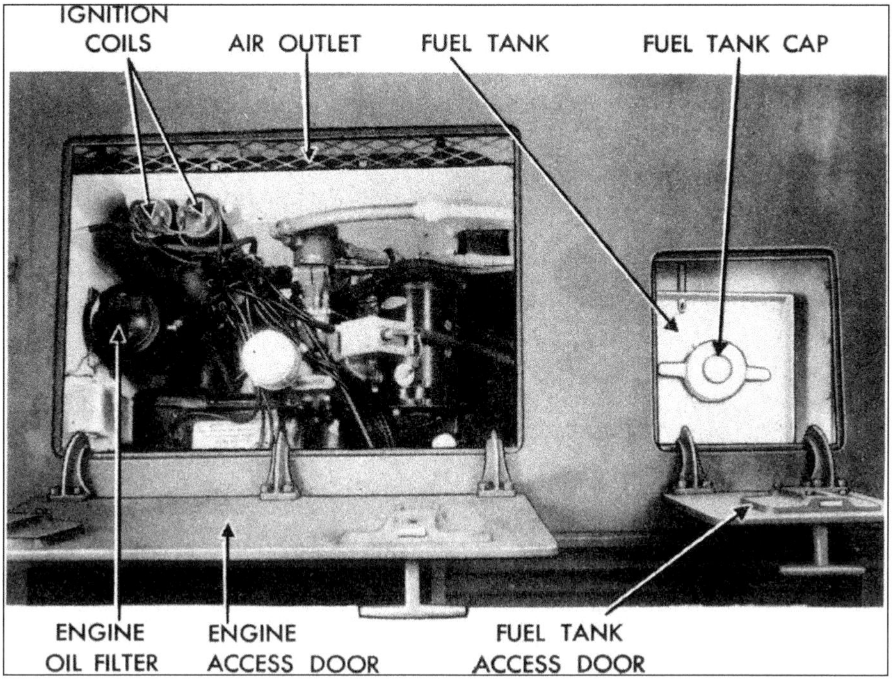

The Lycoming O-435-T tank engine. The O-435-T means opposed six-cylinder engine, 435 cubic inch displacement, tank. This engine was adapted to save weight. To convert the aircraft engine to a tank engine, the following were added: a large blower, a conventional distributor, a large generator and an oil cooler. (TM 9-724, *Light Tank T-9E1*)

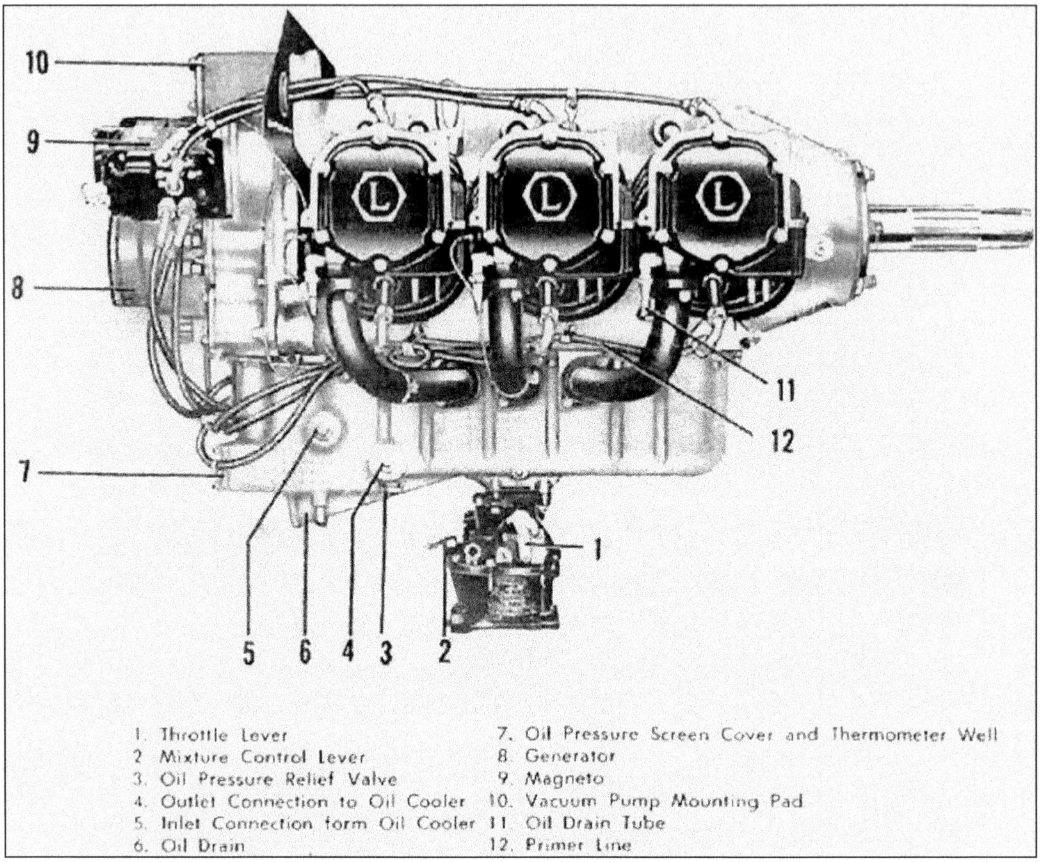

The O-435 aircraft engine. (*Lycoming Model O-435-A Aviation Engine Manual*)

Lycoming O-435-T Engine Specifications

Engine model	O-435-T
Type	horizontally opposed
Number of cylinders	6
Bore	4.875in
Stroke	3.8775in
Firing order	1-4-5-2-3-6
Piston displacement	434 cubic inches
Compression ratio	6.25 to 1
Rated RPM	2,800RPM
Rated brake horsepower at sea level	162HP at 2,800RPM

Crankshaft rotation when viewed from rear	clockwise
Dry weight	755lb
Height of engine	31.28in
Width of engine	35.62in
Length of engine	48.07in
Engine oil	Summer SAE 50, Winter SAE 30
Engine oil sump capacity	6–12 Quarts

The Lycoming O-435 engine was adapted for usage in the tank and redesignated O-435-T. These engines were lightweight, proven in aircraft and available. A distributor was added to replace the original magnetos. The distributor cap had sixteen plug wire connectors and a rotor with two outer clips so that two spark plugs fired simultaneously and independently. The upper and lower ignitions systems were capable of being switched off independently. A large generator was installed that was not original equipment. A large flywheel was attached with fins on the outer diameter to act as a cooling blower. This then mated with the clutch assembly.

The rear view of the engine looking forward toward the driver's position. (TM 9-724, *Light Tank T-9E1*)

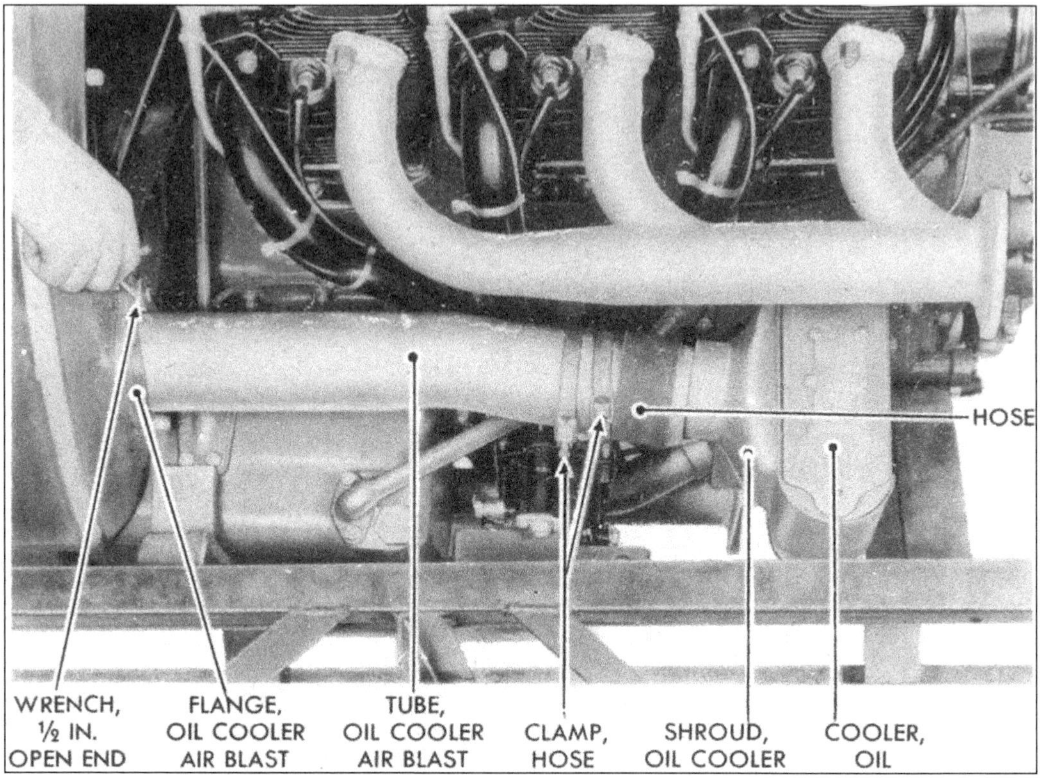

The oil cooler and oil cooler duct which scavenges air from the large cooling fan attached to the flywheel. (TM 9-724, *Light Tank T-9E1*)

The O-435T engine showing the clutch and blower assembly. This blower assembly is necessary for this engine since there is no airflow when compared with an aircraft installation. (TM 9-724, *Light Tank T-9E1*)

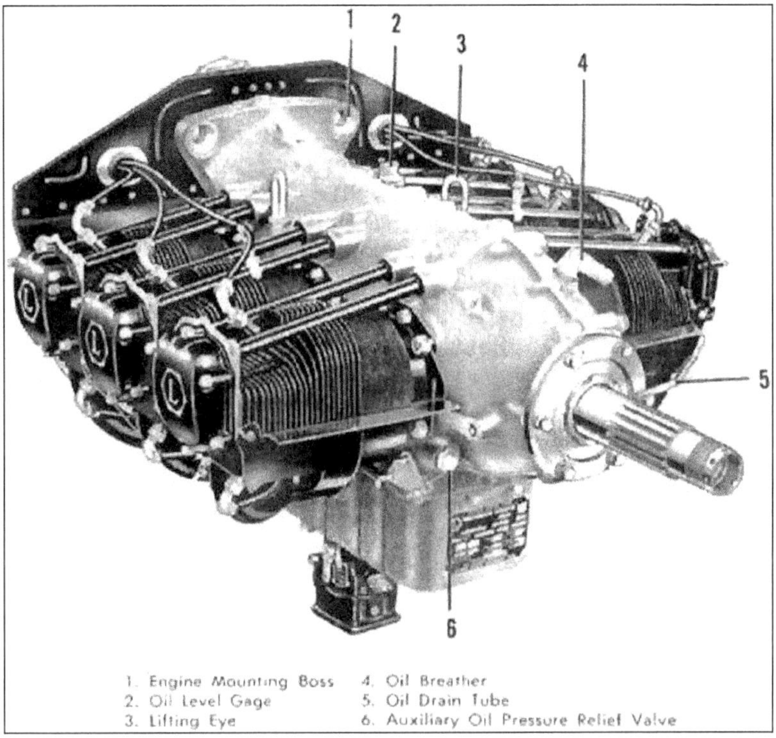

Above: The aircraft version of the Lycoming O-435. (*Lycoming Model O-435-A Aviation Engine Manual*)

Right: Removal of the engine. Certain parts of the engine are easy to work on, others are not. The carburetor is at the bottom of the engine and the only access is a port under the vehicle. Exhaust manifolds are difficult to remove without removing the engine. (TM 9-724, *Light Tank T-9E1*)

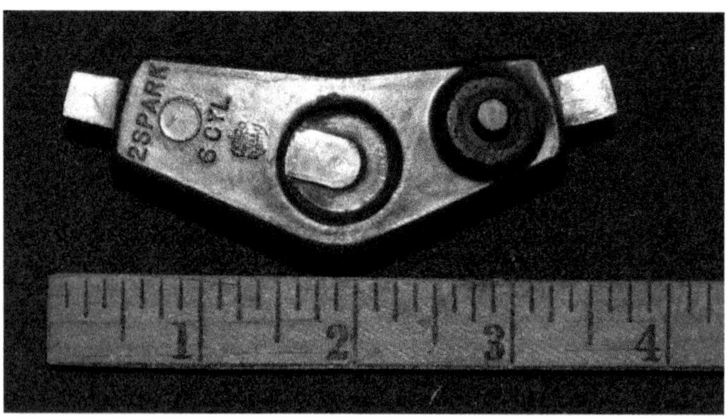

Above and left: The distributor body and rotor. The center contact is for one ignition system. The outer contact is for the second ignition system. (TM 9-724, Light Tank T-9E1)

Above left and right: The distributor cap for the M22 O-435-T engine. It had twelve spark-plug wire outputs and two ignition coil inputs. The notation on the spark-plug outlets read 1U for upper spark plug at cylinder 1, and 1L for lower spark plug for cylinder 1. The two inputs into the distributor are for the dual ignition system. (Roberts Collection)

The carburetor, which is under the engine, being removed. This is difficult when the engine is in the vehicle. (TM 9-724, Light Tank T-9E1)

Filter screens for air inlet into the blower compartment, which is just behind the crew seating. (TM 9-724, *Light Tank T-9E1*)

Opposite above: The exhaust manifold and oil cooler assembly which scavenges air from the blower compartment. Removal of the oil cooler is difficult without engine removal. (TM 9-724, *Light Tank T-9E1*)

The differential and transmission unit. Early transmissions were unreliable, but deficiencies were corrected. (TM 9-724, *Light Tank T-9E1*)

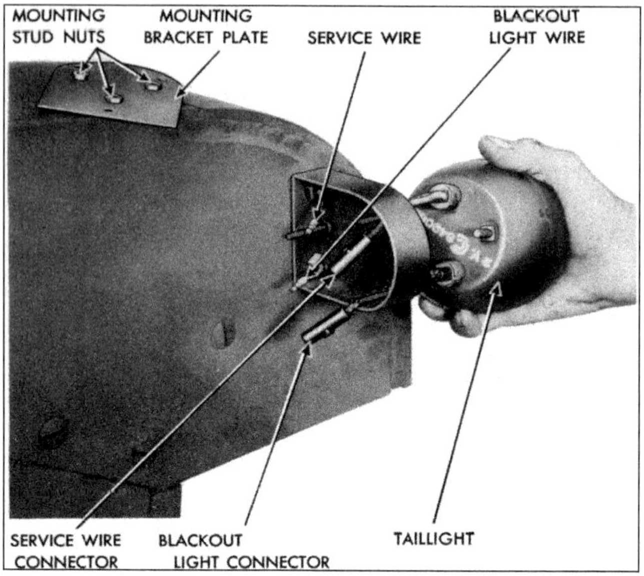

The tail light and scew connectors for removal. (TM 9-724, *Light Tank T-9E1*)

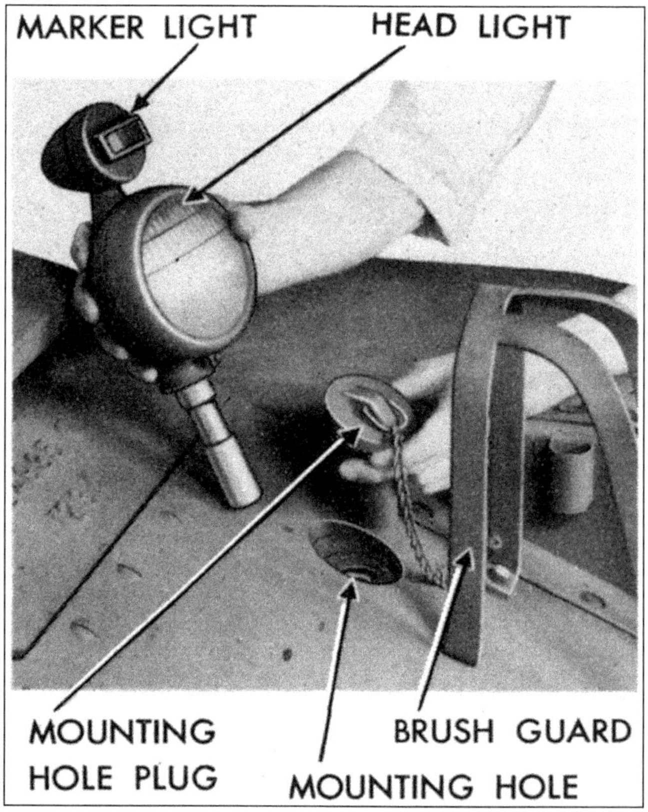

The left headlight and hole plug used when the light is stored inside the vehicle to avoid damage during combat. (TM 9-724, *Light Tank T-9E1*)

Another view of the left headlight assembly and guard. (TM 9-724, *Light Tank T-9E1*)

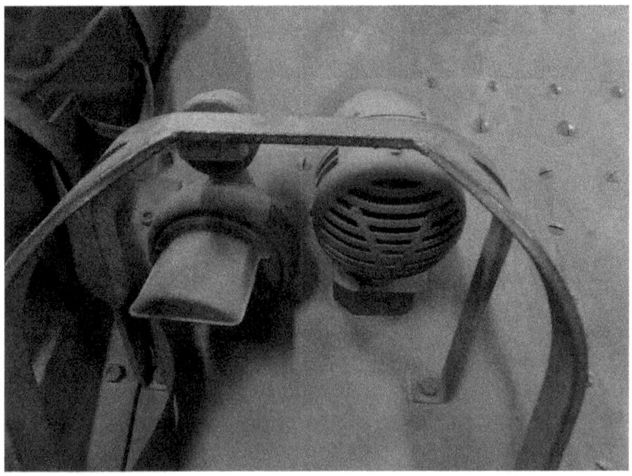

The blackout light assembly and siren. Tanks were typically equipped with sirens as opposed to horns. (Roberts Collection)

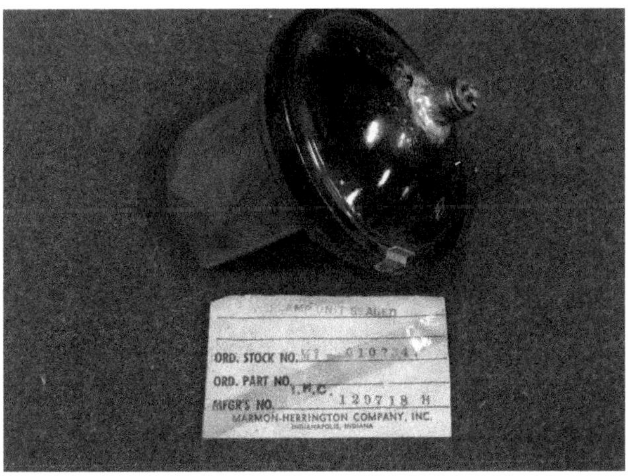

A lamp assembly for the blackout light. (Roberts Collection)

Left: The driver's hatch for an early version of the M22. (Roberts Collection)

Below: The later model tapered hatch which was shaped to reduce weight. (TM 9-724, *Light Tank T-9E1*)

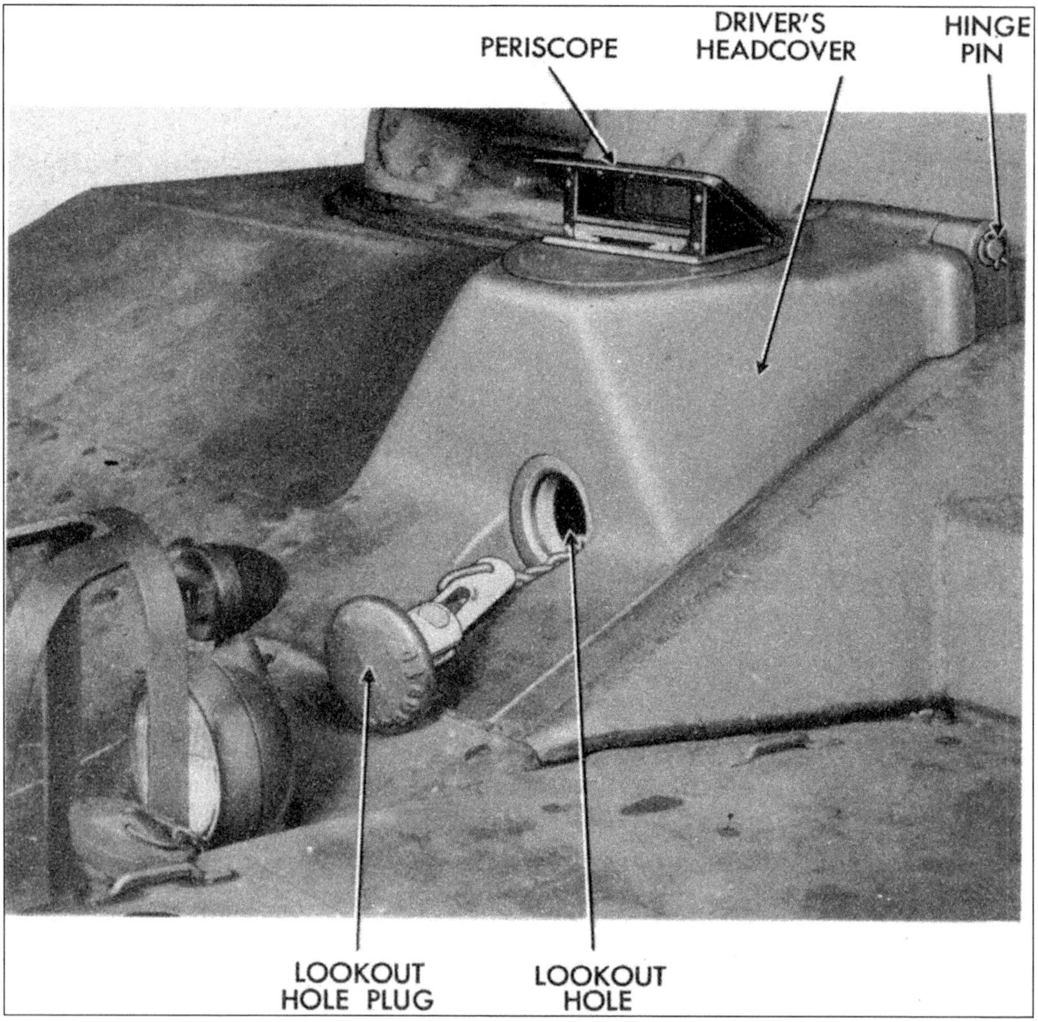

Right: The later model crew compartment showing the M6 periscope slot. The periscope is used in battle to protect the face of the driver. The lookout hole is used in noncombat conditions. (TM 9-724, *Light Tank T-9E1*)

Below: The right side of the vehicle with the lifting lugs used to hoist the hull under a cargo plane. (TM 9-724, *Light Tank T-9E1*)

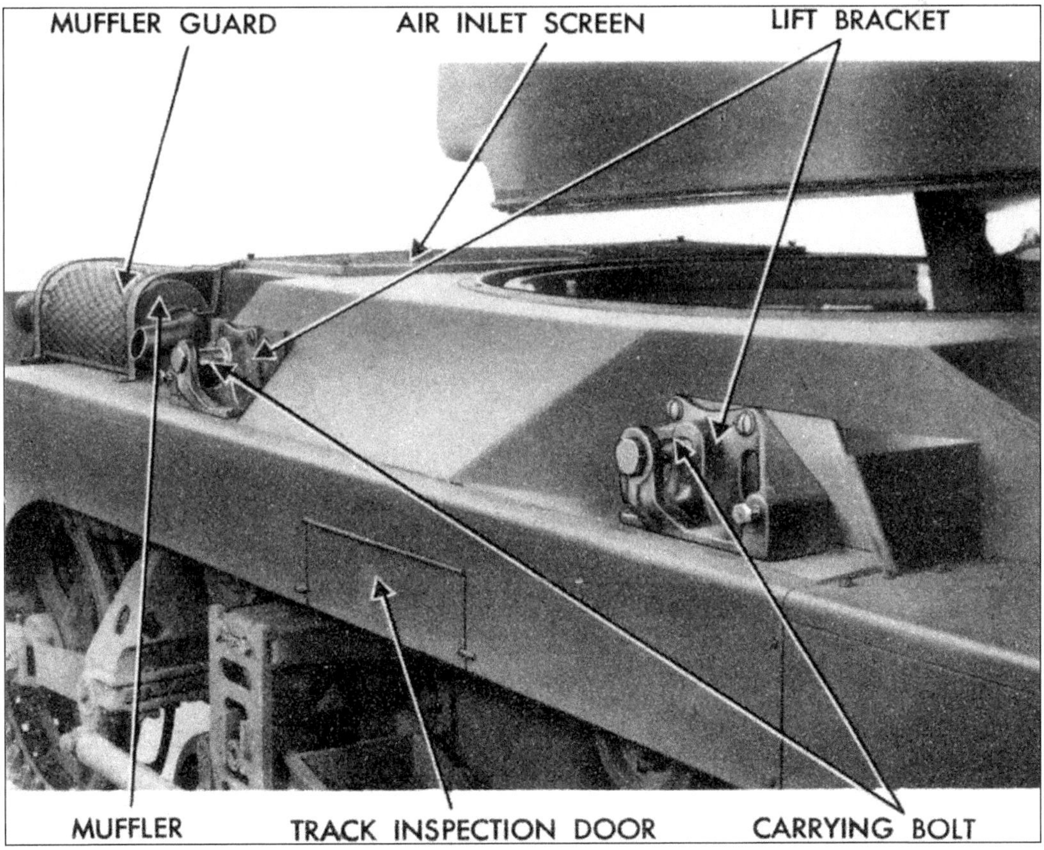

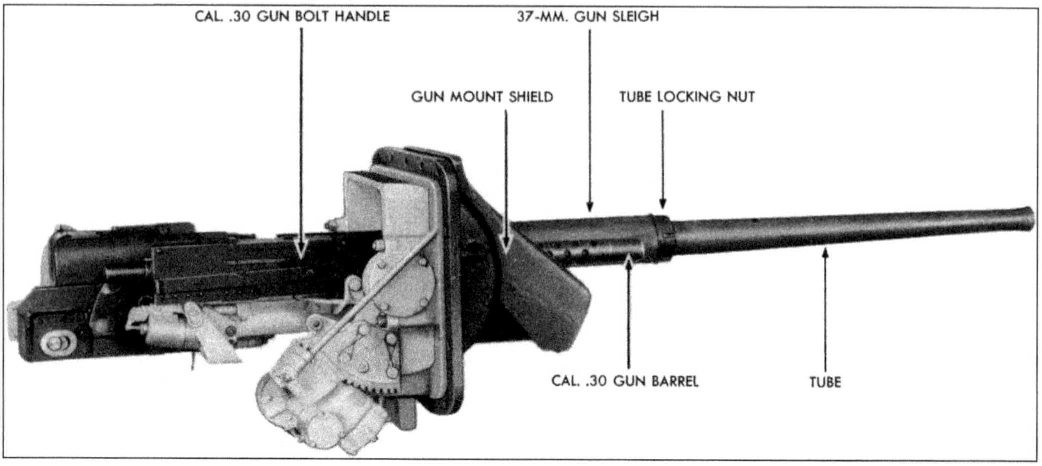

Above, below and opposite: The 37mm tank gun M6. This was also used in the M5 light tank, M8 armored car and M6 37mm gun motor carriage. (FM 23-81, *Basic Field Manual 37-MM Gun, Tank M6 (Mounted in Tanks)*)

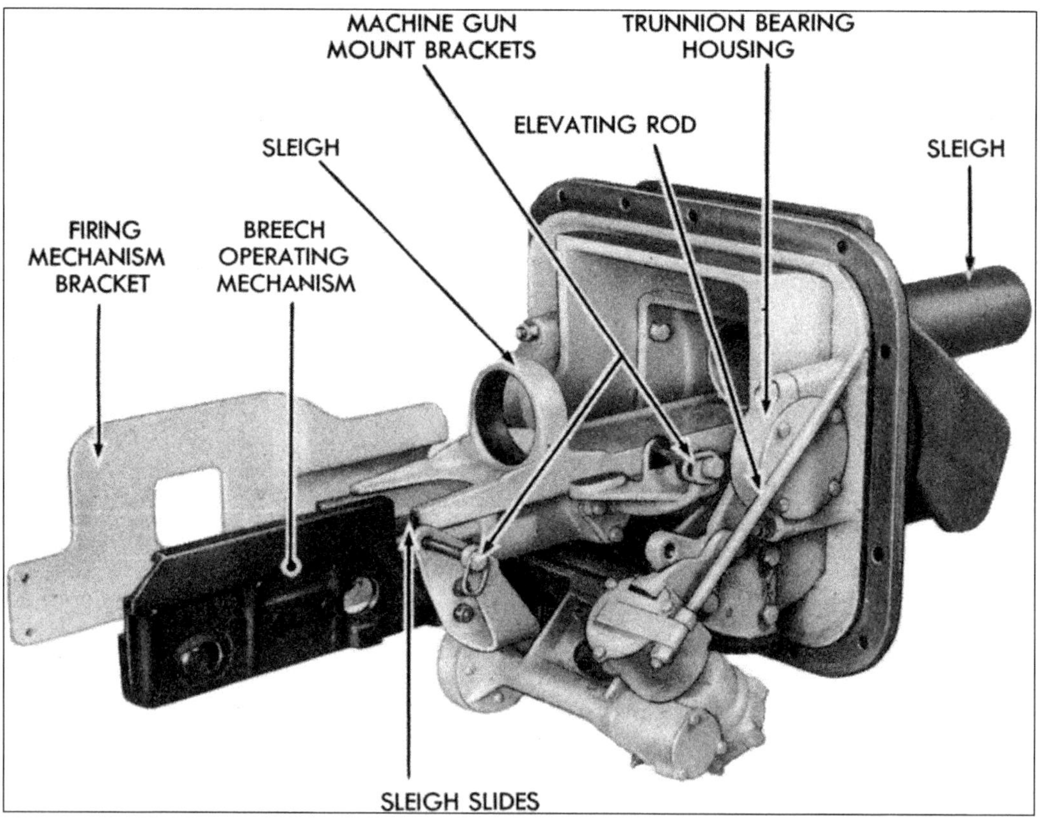

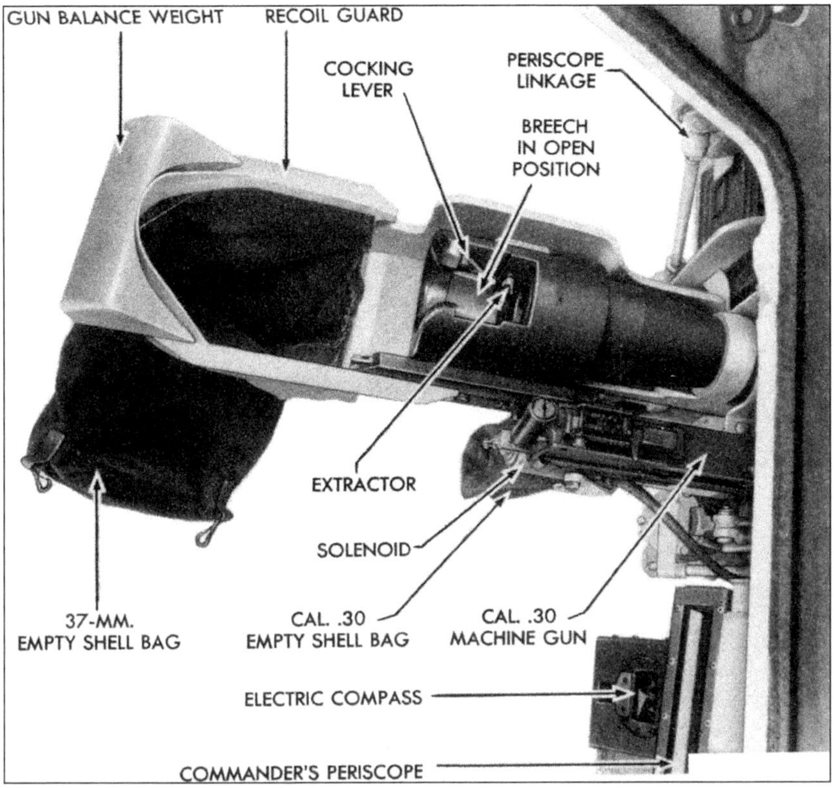
GUN BALANCE WEIGHT
RECOIL GUARD
COCKING LEVER
PERISCOPE LINKAGE
BREECH IN OPEN POSITION
EXTRACTOR
SOLENOID
37-MM. EMPTY SHELL BAG
CAL. .30 EMPTY SHELL BAG
CAL. .30 MACHINE GUN
ELECTRIC COMPASS
COMMANDER'S PERISCOPE

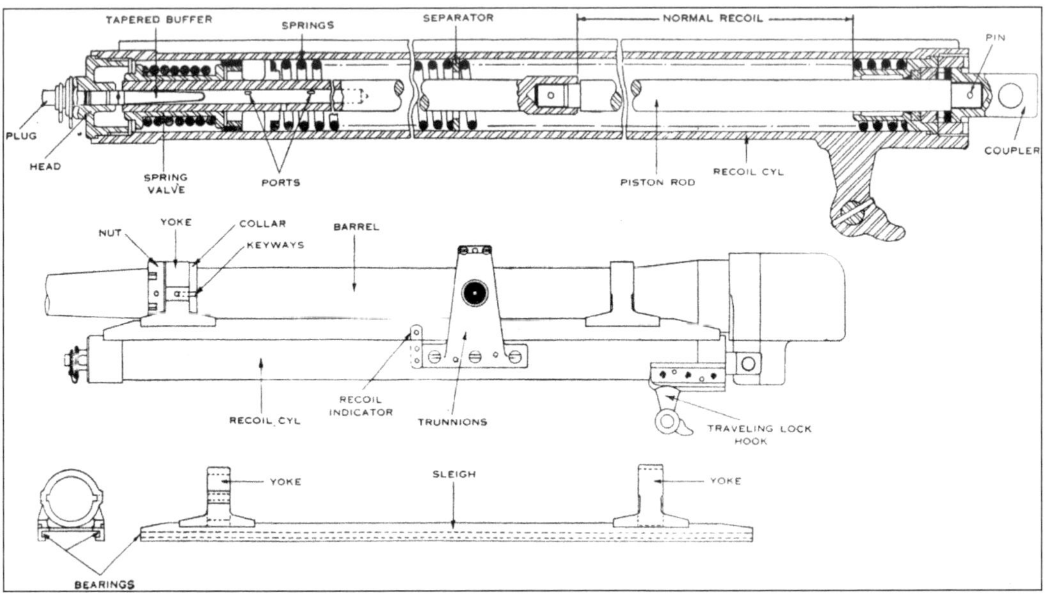
TAPERED BUFFER
SPRINGS
SEPARATOR
NORMAL RECOIL
PIN
PLUG
HEAD
SPRING VALVE
PORTS
PISTON ROD
RECOIL CYL
COUPLER
NUT
YOKE
COLLAR
KEYWAYS
BARREL
RECOIL CYL
RECOIL INDICATOR
TRUNNIONS
TRAVELING LOCK HOOK
YOKE
SLEIGH
YOKE
BEARINGS

Typical ammunition used in the 37mm tank gun is shown on the following pages.

The production schedule for the M22 Locust tank was 100 vehicles per month between August 1943 and January 1944. In February 1944, production was halted because of problems demonstrated during testing. Approximately 830 tanks were produced. In anticipation of deploying the M22 airborne tank, the US Army formed two units: the 151st Airborne Tank Company and the 28th Airborne Tank Battalion.

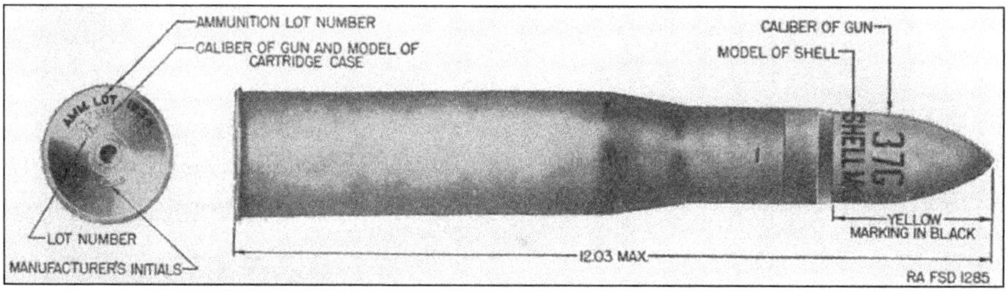

A high-explosive Mk II cartridge with fuse B.D. M38A1. (FM 23-81, *Basic Field Manual 37-MM Gun, Tank M6 (Mounted in Tanks)*)

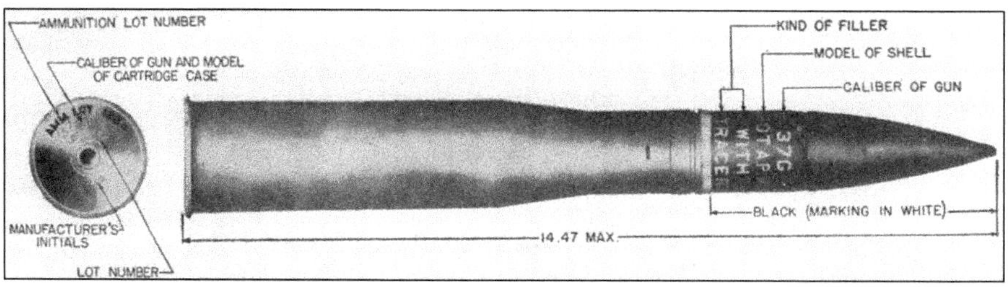

An armor piercing M51 cartridge with tracer. (FM 23-81, *Basic Field Manual 37-MM Gun, Tank M6 (Mounted in Tanks)*)

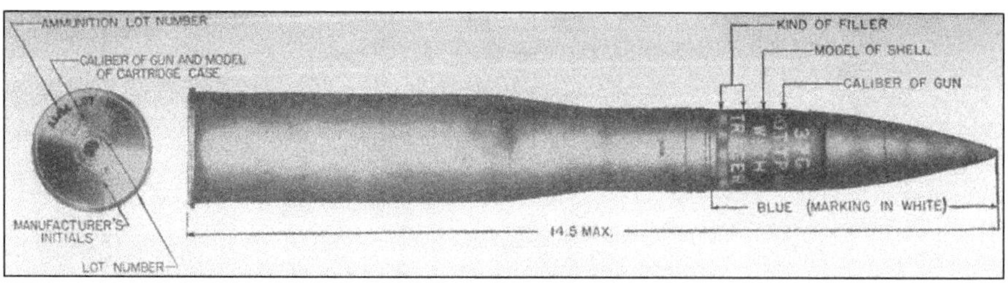

A target-practice M51 cartridge with tracer. (FM 23-81, *Basic Field Manual 37-MM Gun, Tank M6 (Mounted in Tanks)*)

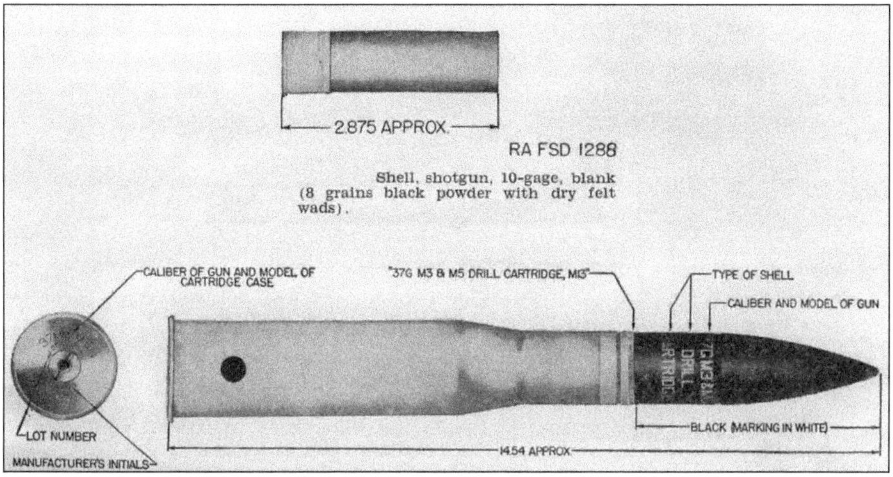

A drill cartridge for training and a shot-gun shell for simulated fire (FM 23-81, *Basic Field Manual 37-MM Gun, Tank M6 (Mounted in Tanks)*)

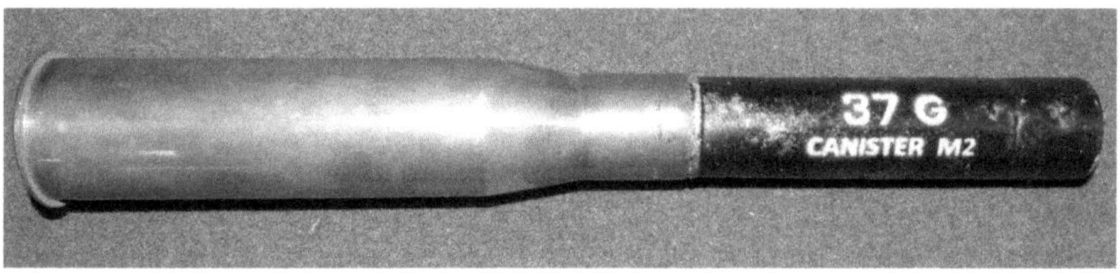

A canister anti-personnel 37G M2 cartridge. (Roberts Collection)

Above and right: An armor piercing M63 cartridge with steel casing. Steel was substituted for brass to save copper, but the performance of the cartridge was inferior. (Roberts Collection)

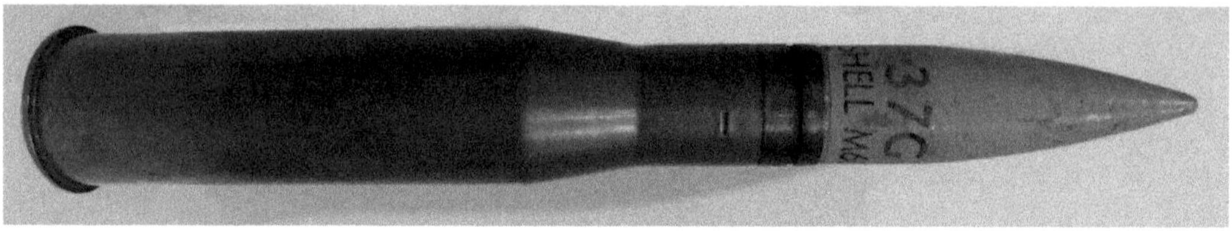

An armor piercing M63 cartridge with brass casing. (Jeff Wszolek Collection)

The fighting compartment in the M22. (TM 9-724, *Light Tank T-9E1*)

Opposite: The M22 used the SCR-510 radio with the RC-99 interphone communication system between crew members. The system operates on a 12-volt source, so any equipment rated for other voltages may be damaged if connected to this source. For instance, if a 6-volt radio set is used, the tubes will probably burn out. Interference with radio transmission is handled by testing the radio noise level when the vehicle engine is running and off. Interference can usually be eliminated by cleaning, tightening or replacing noise producing parts. (TM 11-2705, *Installation of Radio and Interphone Equipment in Light Tank T-9E1*)

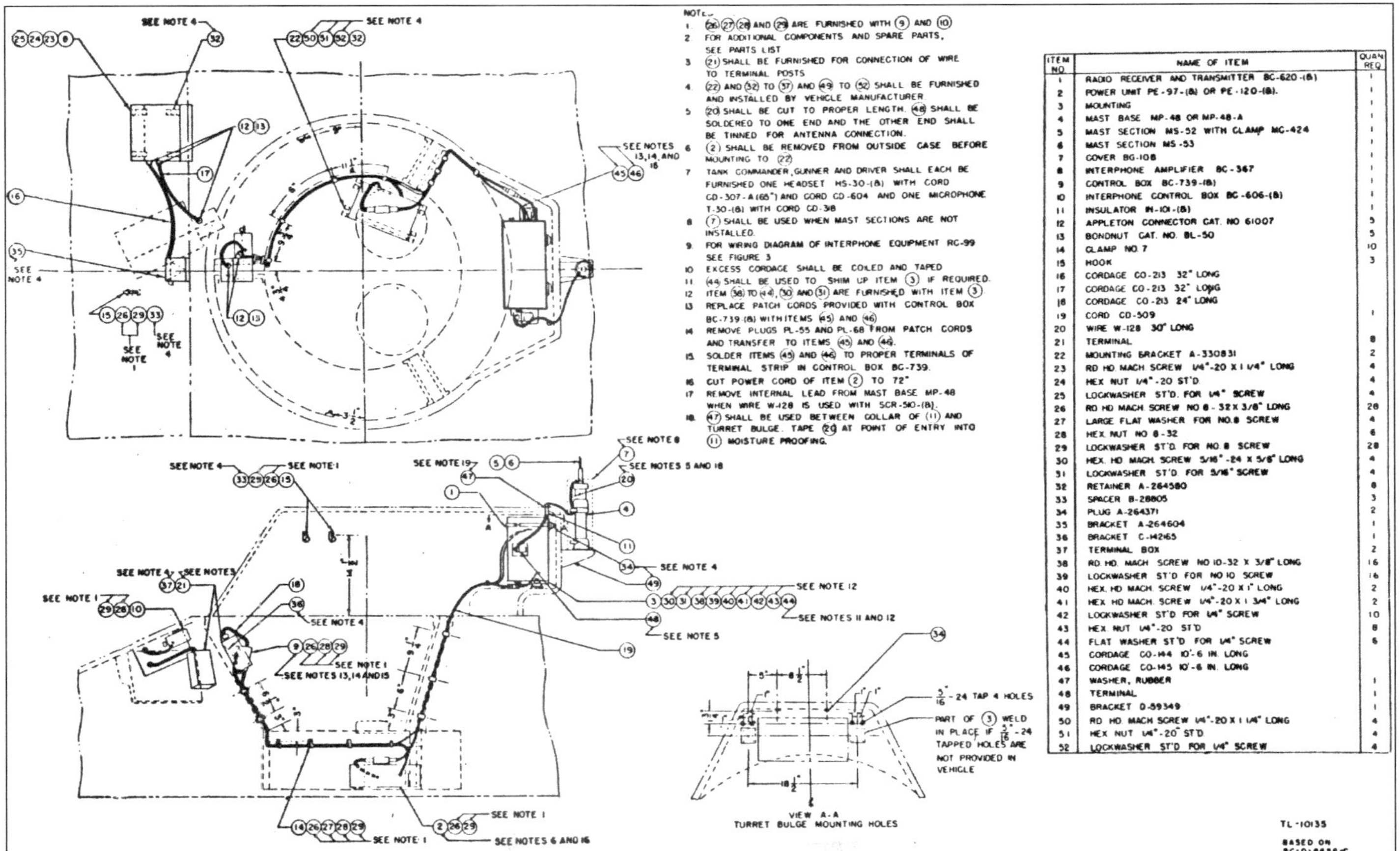

Installation of Radio Set SCR–510–(*) and Interphone Equipment RC–99 in Light Tank T9E1

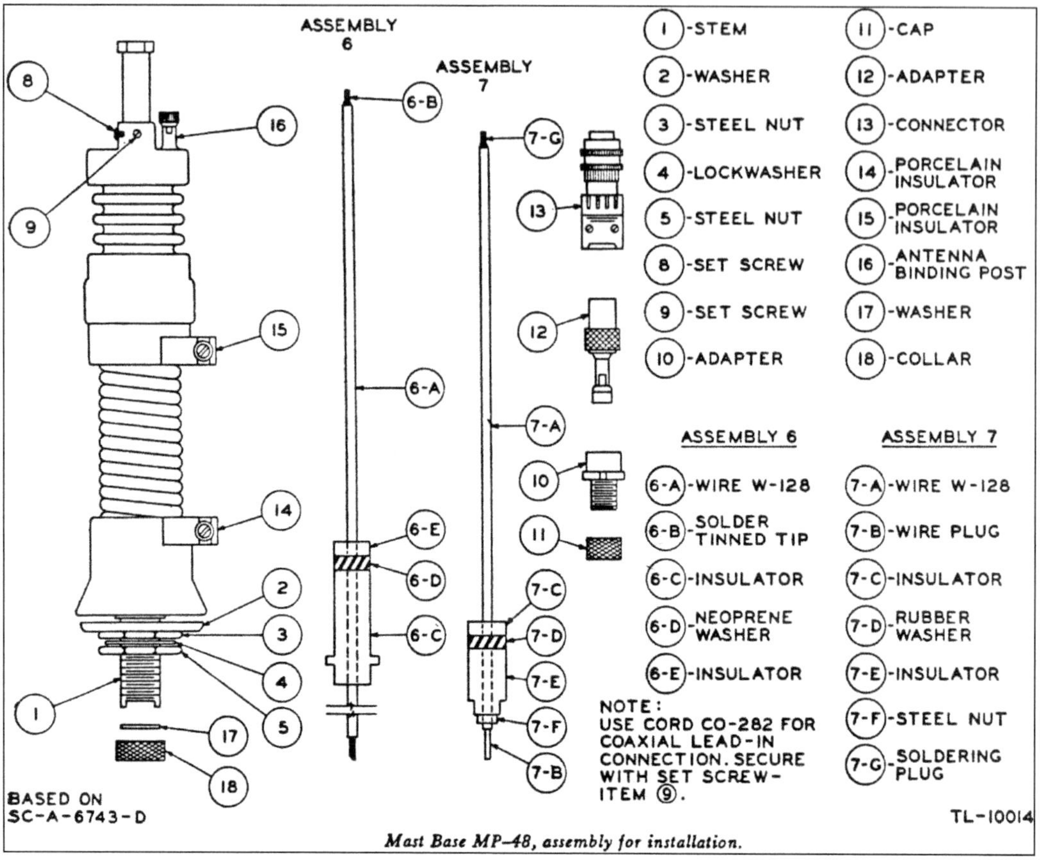

MP-48 radio mast base and associated parts. This was located right behind the turret. (TM 11-2705, *Installation of Radio and Interphone Equipment in Light Tank T-9E1*)

Opposite above: Experimental M22 prime mover for towing an anti-tank gun. (US Army Signal Corps)

Opposite below: M22 Serial Number 110. (Roberts Collection)

USA 3067110

Chapter 3

The 151st Airborne Tank Company and the 28th Airborne Tank Battalion in the Second World War

With the development of the T-9 prototype and the eventual M22 light tank, it became necessary to form a unit that would act as the crew. On 15 August 1943, five officers and seventy enlisted men were assigned to Fort Knox, Kentucky, to form the first United States airborne tank unit of the Second World War. Headquarters Armored Command GO #77, dated 6 August 1943, authorized the activation of this unit, designated the 151st Airborne Tank Company. The command structure was as follows:

Company Commander: Captain Arthur Gremillion

Junior officers: 1st Lieutenants Richard McCabe, William Tipton, Herman Rosenberg and 2nd Lieutenant Kenneth Gross

Enlisted: 1st Sergeant George C. Norton, Staff Sergeants Jenkins Smith, Ewert Varney, Gabriele Sciabarasi, Frank McGrath, Burnie Peland, J.C. Grider and Charles Shepherd

These men were volunteers from the 20th Armored Division in Camp Campbell, Kentucky. They were selected to form this unique US Army unit – glider tankers. The company immediately began individual training (IT) where each person attended classes and exercises on basic military science. On 28 August, twenty-two enlisted men were assigned to the 151st, authorized by GO #146. By the end of August when it reached its T/O (table of organization) strength, additional soldiers had

BATTALION TYPE:	T/O-Table of Organization	Officers	Warrant Officers	Enlisted Men	Medium Tank	Medium Tank w/105mm Howitzer	Medium Tank, Special	Light Tank	75mm Howitzer, motor carriage	75mm Pack Howitzer	Halftrack, 81mm Mortar M21	Rocket Launcher, 2.75" Anti-Tank	Machine gun, .50 cal	Machine gun, .30 cal	Submachinegun, .45 cal	Carbine, .30 cal	Pistol, .45 cal	Halftrack, M3 Personnel	Halftrack, M3 Ambulance	Truck, 2½ - ton	Truck, ¾ - ton Command & Reconnaissance	Truck, ¾ - ton Weapons Carrier	Truck, ¼ - ton	Wrecker, Heavy	Tank Recovery Vehicle, T5	81mm Mortar
Tank Battalion	17-25 (15 Sep 43)	39	2	709	53	6	-	17	-	-	3	35	26	18	449	277	3	13	3	39	1	1	23	2	6	6
Medium, special	17-45 S (4 Dec. 43)	32	2	609	18	-	54	-	-	-	-	27	20	16	439	240	3	9	3	39	2	1	24	2	5	5
Light Tank Bn.	17-15 (12 Nov 43)	34	2	513	-	-	-	59	3	-	3	22	17	9	293	237	3	12	2	23	1	1	21	2	-	-
Airborne Tank Bn.	17-55 (15 Jan 44)	27	3	356	-	-	-	56	-	3	-	8	23	22	211	159	3	-	-	-	-	13	41	-	-	-

Table of Organization T/O for Second World War American tank units. (Stanton, *Order of Battle: U.S. Army, World War II*)

arrived from the 20th Armored Division, the Armored School and the Demonstration Regiment, all at Fort Knox, Kentucky.

The 28th Airborne Tank Battalion was activated on 6 December 1943 according to GO #2. The 28th was a larger unit to accommodate the production of more airborne tanks and their crews. The initial command structure is as follows on 6 December 1943:

Battalion Commander: Major Everett I. Bibb

Captains: Captain Scott H. Braznell (Adjutant), Captain Thomas F. Moore, Captain Gerald W. Scurry (Medical Officer)

Lieutenants: 1st Lieutenant Donald C. Lusk, 1st Lieutenant Floyd A. Northrop, 1st Lieutenant Louis A. Paleo, 2nd Lieutenant Harry T. Lee, 2nd Lieutenant James L. Suntum

Warrant Officer Junior Grade: Frank J. McGrath

These officers were volunteers from the 16th Armored Division, the 20th Armored Division and the 785th Tank Battalion.

On 8 December, 1st Lieutenant John Parson and 2nd Lieutenant George A. Soloman joined the company. On 12 December 1943, Captain Gremillion was assigned to the newly formed 28th Airborne Tank Battalion. 1st Lieutenant McCabe assumed command and 2nd Lieutenant James L. Suntum joined the company. On 16 December, the IT program ended, two days later the IT tests were given to the tankers in the unit, and all passed. On 24 December 1943, 1st Lieutenant McCabe was transferred to the 28th Airborne Tank Battalion, and 1st Lieutenant Parson assumed command of the company. On the same day, Staff Sergeant Grider was sent to the 28th Airborne Tank Battalion and Staff Sergeant Yeates joined the company from that battalion.

On 25 December, the 151st Airborne Tank Company started the second phase of training with tank gunnery. Lieutenant Elvin Bess from the Armored Replacement Training Center arrived to direct the gunnery training.

Tank gunnery training lasted approximately twenty-seven weeks. The first phase, which was fifteen weeks in duration, involved equipment care and maintenance, crew drill, simulated direct fire, range and speed estimation, ammunition, sub-caliber direct firing, a proficiency test and direct firing with live ammunition. The second phase was twelve weeks and covered platoon level direct firing, drill for indirect firing with single tank, live indirect firing with single tank, drill for indirect firing with two or more tanks, live indirect firing with

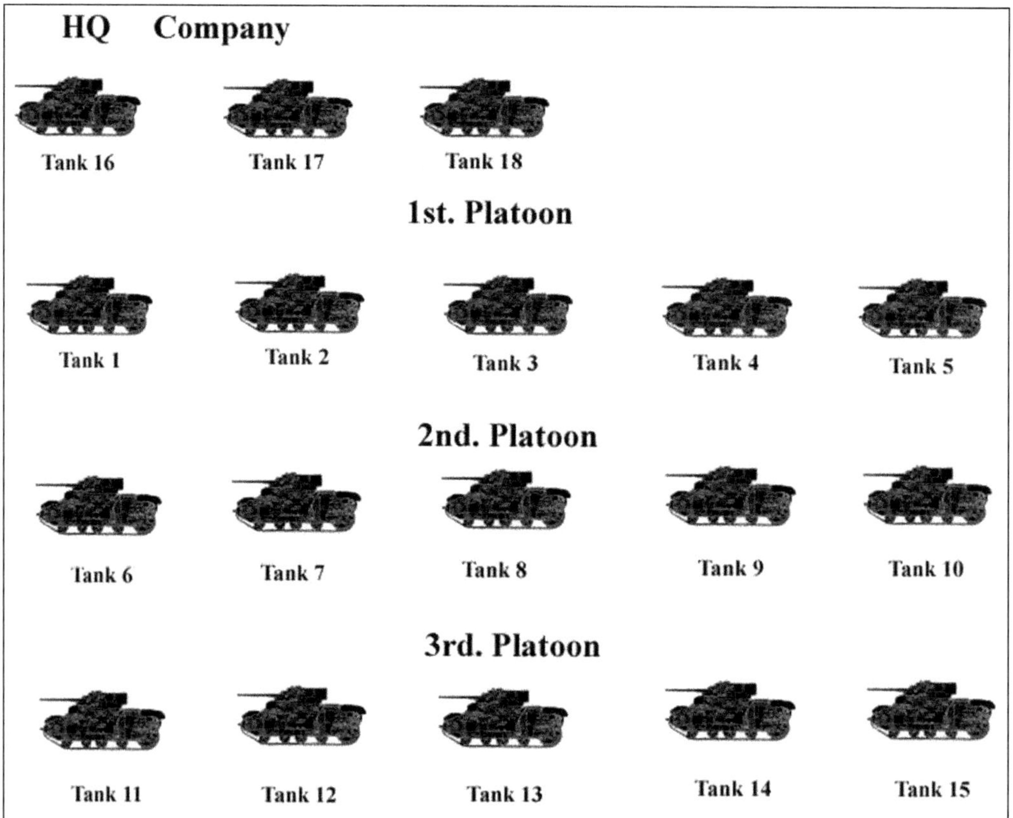

151st Airborne Tank Company command structure.

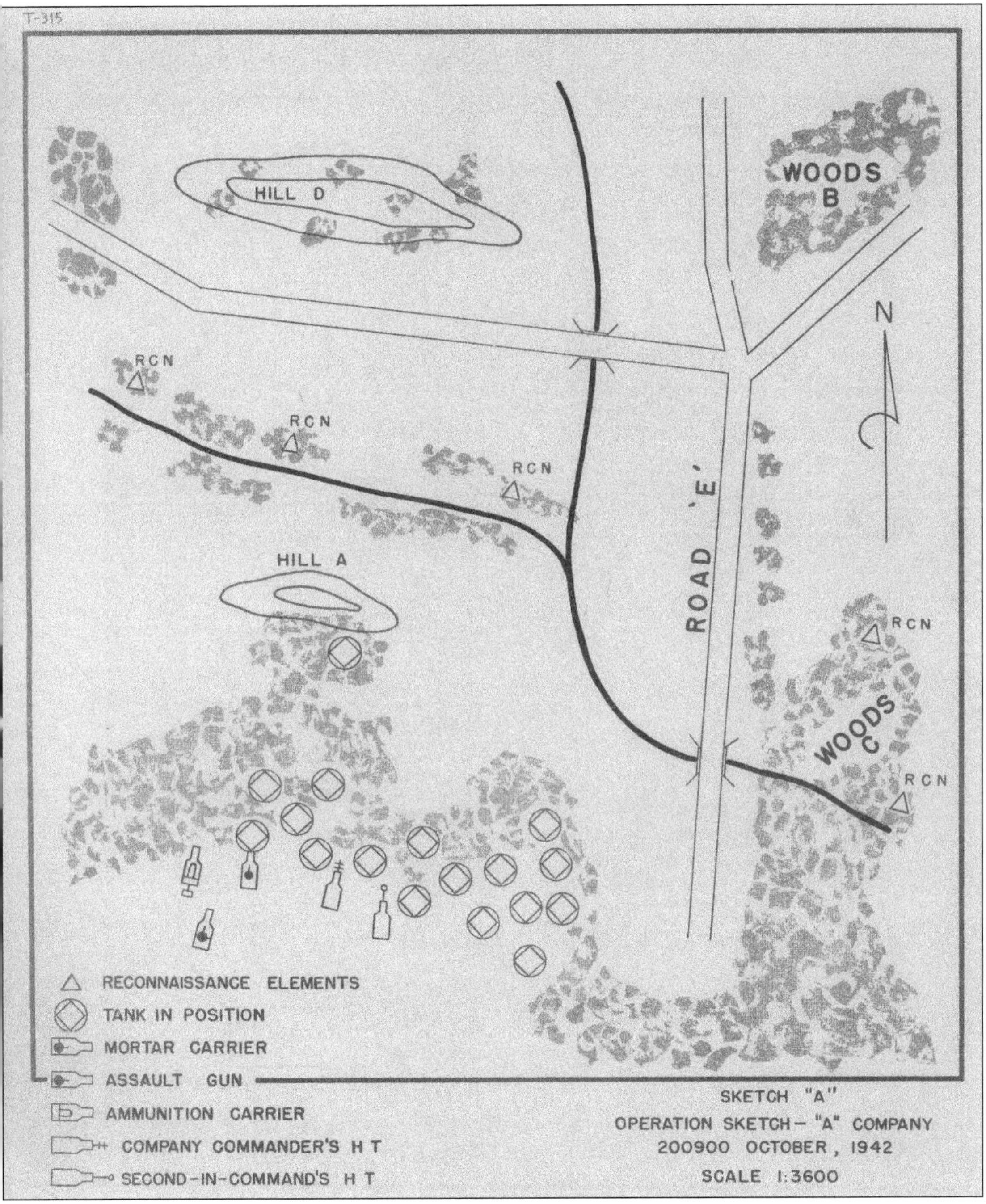

Practice field map used in training with respect to combat orders. (T-315, *Combat Orders*)

Above left and right: 151st Airborne Tank Company at Fort Knox, Kentucky, 1943. (Sacquety, 'The 151st Airborne Tank Company at Camp Mackall, NC'; The American Society of Military Insignia Collectors)

151st Airborne Tank Company at Fort Knox, Kentucky, 1943. (Hughes, 'The 151st Airborne Tank Company')

Above: The 28th Airborne Tank Battalion Headquarters Company (Roberts Collection)

Right: First Platoon and Company Commander (seated right) of an airborne tank company of the 28th Airborne Tank Battalion. (Roberts Collection)

Second Platoon of an airborne tank company of the 28th Airborne Tank Battalion. (Roberts Collection)

Third Platoon of an airborne tank company of the 28th Airborne Tank Battalion. Lieutenant August Dreier, platoon leader, is seated. (Roberts Collection)

Above left and right: Patch arrangement for the 151st Airborne Tank Company which was essentially the armor unassigned patch and the airborne rocker above. (Roberts Collection)

Below: Glider badge worn by Lieutenant August Dreier, platoon leader, 28th Airborne Tank Battalion. (Roberts Collection)

Left: Sergeant Patrick Dailey of the 151st with armor unassigned patch and airborne rocker. (Sacquety, 'The 151st Airborne Tank Company at Camp Mackall, NC')

Below left: Patch and rocker for the 28th Airborne Tank Battalion. (David Kaufman Collection)

Below right: Patch and rocker for the 151st Airborne Tank Company. (Roberts Collection)

Above: Close-up of a crash helmet with R-14 head set and PL-55 plug to the tank communication circuit. The throat microphone is clearly seen. (Roberts Collection)

Right: A tanker combat uniform comprising herringbone twill (HBT) coveralls with a tanker helmet (crash helmet). (Roberts Collection)

Below: Three tank-crew members with armor patch sewn on the left breast of the coverall. The jackets had the armor patch on the left shoulder like other US Army units. (The American Society of Military Insignia Collectors)

Tarpaper barracks at Camp Mackall, 1944. (Sacquety, 'The 151st Airborne Tank Company at Camp Mackall, NC')

Jeep of the Reconnaissance Platoon at Camp Mackall, 1944. Private William Rasbolt is sitting in the passenger seat. The bumper identification is Airborne Command 151st Airborne Tank Company. (Sacquety, 'The 151st Airborne Tank Company at Camp Mackall, NC')

An M22 of the 151st Airborne Tank Company at Fort Knox, Kentucky, 1943. This image illustrates the fragility of the sand skirts. They typically were damaged when traveling through forests, catching small trees and stumps, and the rear one in particular when material became engaged in the idler wheel and rotated upward. The flap on the sand skirt, just under the star, allows access to the track for adjustment and inspection. (Hughes, 'The 151st Airborne Tank Company')

This M22 of the 151st appears to be equipped with a field expedient. There is a protective shield attached to the driver's hatch. While in convoy, the hatch is typically open, which allows debris to enter the driver's compartment. The M5A1 light tank had a detachable windshield as standard equipment. (Sacquety, 'The 151st Airborne Tank Company at Camp Mackall, NC')

Members of a platoon of the 28th Airborne Tank battalion at a firing range, possibly at Fort Campbell, Kentucky. Four M22 light tanks can be seen in the background. The white rectangles on the right of the photograph appear to be practice targets. (Roberts Collection)

Tanker of the 151st in combat uniform with a Thompson submachine gun. (Sacquety, 'The 151st Airborne Tank Company at Camp Mackall, NC')

Above and below: M22 tanks and crews during training maneuvers, 1944. (Sacquety, 'The 151st Airborne Tank Company at Camp Mackall, NC')

Above and below: These drawings depict the importance of tank machine-gun attacks on enemy positions. (FM 17-12, *Armored Force Field Manual, Tank Gunnery*)

two or more tanks, combat firing of small units and combat firing of large units. The Armored Force Field Manual on Tank Gunnery stated: 'The ultimate objective of the armored division is vital rear installations. These are attacked less with cannon than with crushing power of the tank and with its machine guns.'* This reflected the doctrine that tanks are to support infantry and tank destroyers are to deal with other tanks.

There were a number of steps in the tank gunnery training received by the 151st. The first step was operation and handling of equipment. The students became familiar with the tank and its systems to the satisfaction of the instructor. The goal was to instill a sense of responsibility for taking care of the tank, weapons and systems. Careless operation was severely disciplined.

The second step in training was making tank crews realize that the proper operation of their equipment was a life and death matter. A preventable malfunction of a gun could mean the enemy got the first shot, which could be decisive. Leadership training was also provided. The platoon leader made daily inspections for general appearance and spot checked critical components for proper functioning. The platoon leader checked maintenance records for proper lubrication intervals and documentation.

The third step in tank gunnery training was the crew drill. This exercise helped the crew to act as a team and become adept at movement around the tank. The top image of the tank crew drill (on the following page) shows the crew at attention in front of their vehicle ready for inspection. The lower image shows the crew mounting the tank into their assigned positions. This was a generic procedure for the medium tank. The M22 tank would have had three crew members doing essentially the same drill. The crew was rated on their ability to quickly fall in, and on command to quickly mount the tank in their assigned positions.

The fourth step dealt with simulated firing. The crew was drilled on how to prepare for action. Several simulated firing problems were presented and after completion, the tank was removed from the firing range. Crews were also drilled on how and when to abandon the tank.

The fifth step in crew gunnery training was range and speed estimation of the target. Range estimation was necessary for the correct elevation of the main gun. Speed estimation determined the proper sighting lead so that the projectile arrived at the same location of the moving target at the same time. Every time the tank was moved a new range estimation was calculated. Also, when a moving target was acquired a new lead was calculated. Practice on determining the range of the target would be accomplished with gunsights, tank periscopes,

* FM 17-12, *Armored Force Field Manual, Tank Gunnery,* War Department, 22 April 1943.

Tank crew drill. (FM 17-12, *Armored Force Field Manual, Tank Gunnery*)

Direct laying or direct firing is the condition where a tank gunner can view the target through the gunsight and fire directly at it, as seen here. The tank is also in defilade mode where the hull is down in a ditch and minimally exposed to return fire from the enemy. (FM 17-12, *Armored Force Field Manual, Tank Gunnery*)

Indirect laying or indirect firing is the condition where a tank gunner cannot see the target which is typically obscured by terrain. The gunner must rely on a forward observer, as seen to the left of the tank in the drawing, to obtain information on the elevation and azimuth. The forward observer then relays correction to the trajectory, if necessary, to hit the target. (FM 17-12, *Armored Force Field Manual, Tank Gunnery*)

field glasses and the naked eye. It should be noted that target range would be under estimated when:

1. In bright light.
2. The target contrasted significantly with the background color.
3. The target was observed over water, snow or a flat field.
4. Looking down a straight road or railroad track.
5. Looking down from a height.
6. Looking over a depression.

Target range was often overestimated when:

1. There was poor light, fog or rain.
2. Looking from low ground to higher ground.
3. A small part of the target was visible.

Crews were drilled on various speed estimates: slow (below 10mph), medium (10–20mph) and fast (20mph +). Several military vehicles would be driven on a range at various speeds and distances. Crews were tested on their ability to estimate speed and range of a vehicle.

The sixth step in crew training dealt with ammunition. There was instruction on high explosive (HE), armor piercing (AP), canister and target practice (TP) ammunition. Drills were performed for inspecting ammunition for defects, storing the ammunition in the vehicle, loading practice rounds and loading the proper ammunition for a particular target.

The seventh step in tank gunnery training was firing on a range using sub-caliber firing with 0.30 caliber ammunition. An adapter was used in the main gun that would accept a smaller round than that of the main gun to save on ammunition. It allowed gunners to hone their aiming skills but did not give the sensation of recoil from 37mm ammunition live firing. The firing would occur on ranges up to 800yd. Actual tanks would be used as practice targets since the sub-caliber ammunition would not cause damage and gunners would get more realistic training. For moving targets, tanks would drive over a hilly course to test the gunners' skill in leading and ranging the target.

The eighth step involved a proficiency test before service ammunition was used. There were two parts to the test: a written portion and a demonstration of proficiency in loading the main gun, sighting and disassembly of the breech mechanism and other parts of the main gun.

The ninth step was basic firing on one fixed and one moving target. The number of rounds used was limited due to ammunition shortage at the time. The tenth step was platoon drills using direct laying (direct firing). The platoon leader coordinated simulated fire in platoon formation, not as individual tanks. The platoon leader directed the unit to concentrate fire on a single target at ranges up to 1,000yd. The eleventh step was platoon direct firing using machine guns or sub-caliber ammunition in the main gun. The direct fire was concentrated on a single target. The twelfth step was indirect laying (indirect fire like a howitzer) with a single tank. An observer directed the tank commander on the proper elevation and azimuth for indirect fire simulation. The thirteenth step was mixing of simulated direct fire and simulated indirect fire to test the flexibility of the crew to adapt to each mode of operation. The fourteenth step was indirect laying of two or more tanks in preparation for live firing. The fifteenth step was indirect firing with live service ammunition and evaluating the accuracy. The sixteenth step was combat firing between small units of tanks using coaxial machine guns to simulate the main gun of a tank. All tanks were buttoned up and vulnerable equipment such as headlights removed. This also helped crews get experience in determining where the enemy was located based on the machine-gun hits. The final step was coordinated firing using tanks, mortars, assault guns, anti-tank guns and artillery on the 1,000yd range. The 151st Airborne Tank Company also received training on the technical details of main gun adjustments, aiming calibration and range estimation.

On the 37mm main gun, the front boresight was constructed using thread. At the muzzle end of the gun were grooves that located the thread so that it formed a cross, which is the front boresight as shown in the top, right-hand drawing on the next page, and also shown to the left on an actual tank. The breech end boresight is shown in the top drawing on p. 94. The gunner looked though the peep hole and aligned the gun tube with the target. When aligned, the main gunsight was adjusted to the same point on the target.*

A major component of the training undertaken by the 151st tank crews was proficiency in the various combat-simulation courses. Driving and gunnery skills using sub-caliber and normal ammunition refined tank-crew member skills. Also, platoon leaders and company commanders could exercise the leadership and command required to successfully engage an enemy position. Radio communication was paramount and

* FM 23-81, *Basic Field Manual 37-MM Gun, Tank M6 (Mounted in Tanks)*, War Department, 3 April 1942.

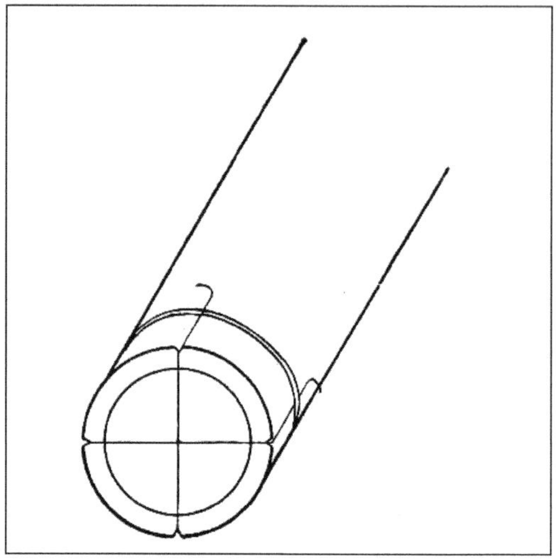

Above left: The muzzle-end boresight for a 37mm gun. (Roberts Collection)

Above right: The front boresight for a 37mm gun. (FM 23-81, *Basic Field Manual 37-MM Gun, Tank M6 (Mounted in Tanks)*)

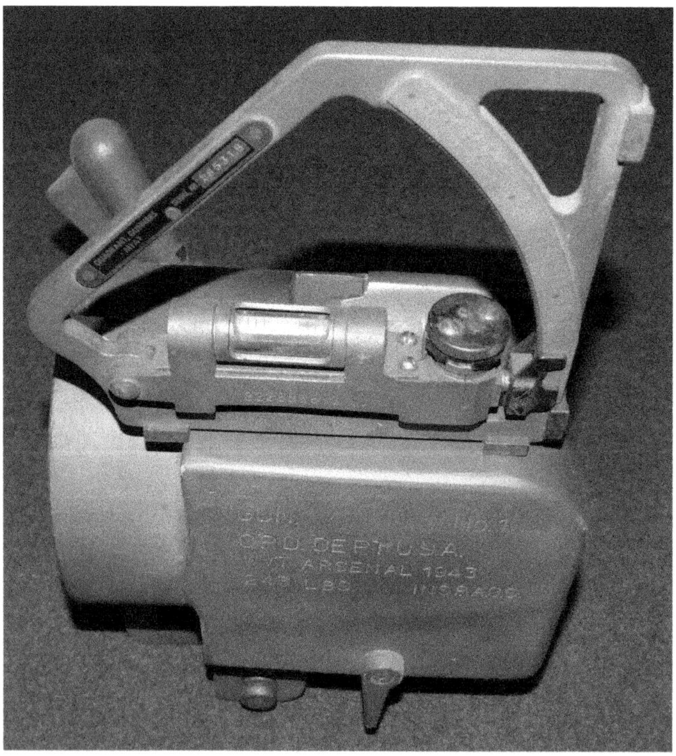

Gunner's quadrant M1 is shown mounted on the breech. This is used to adjust the elevating mechanism of the main gun. If the elevation mechanism is damaged, the gunner's quadrant can be used to lay the proper elevation of the main gun. (Roberts Collection)

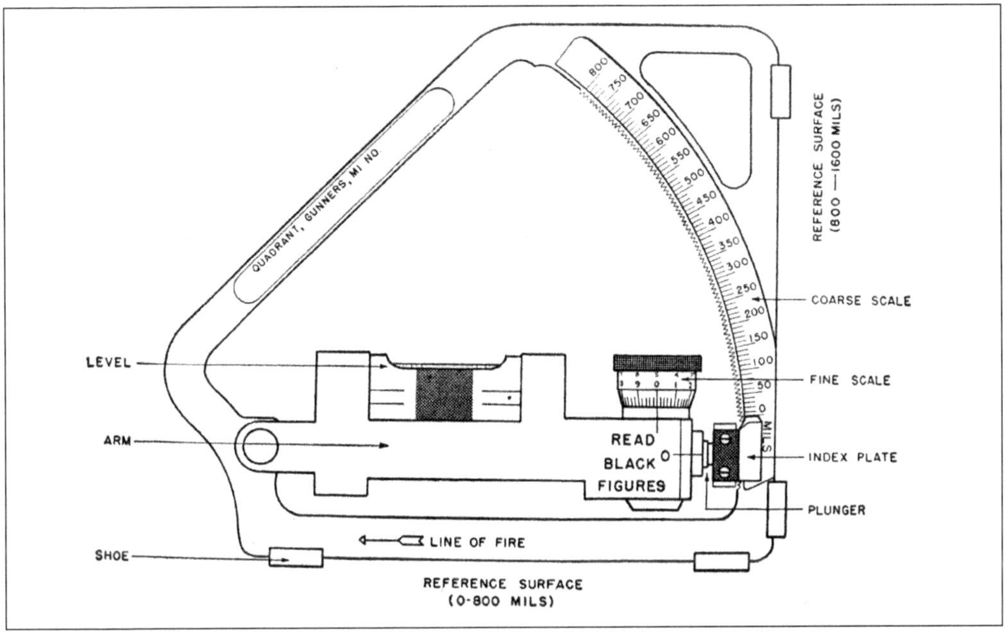

Above and below: Drawing and photograph of gunner's quadrant. (Roberts Collection)

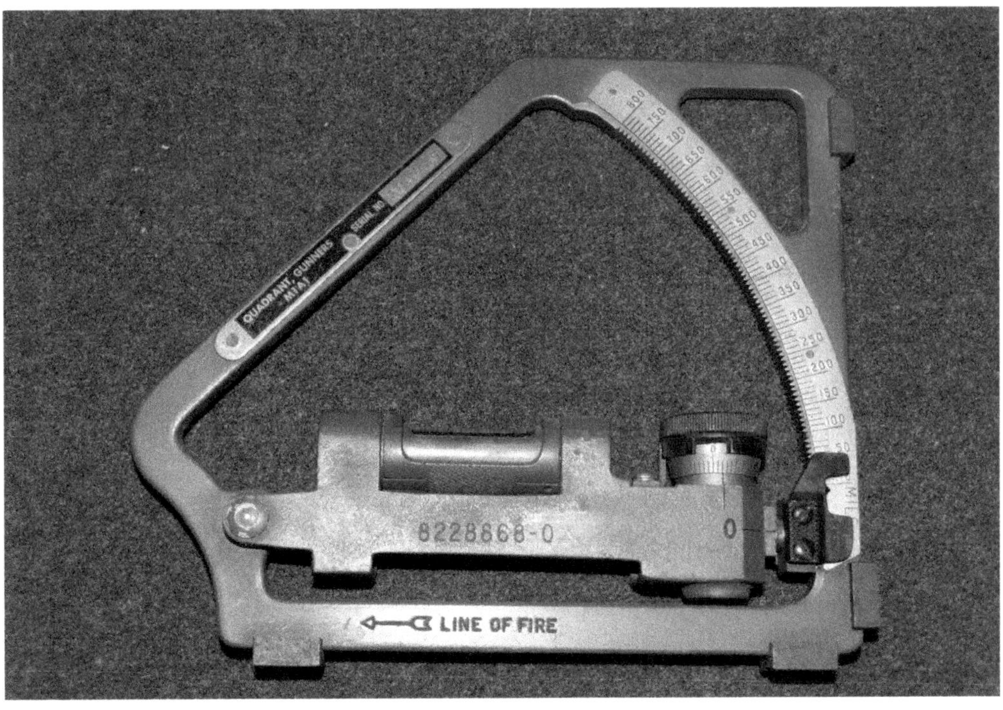

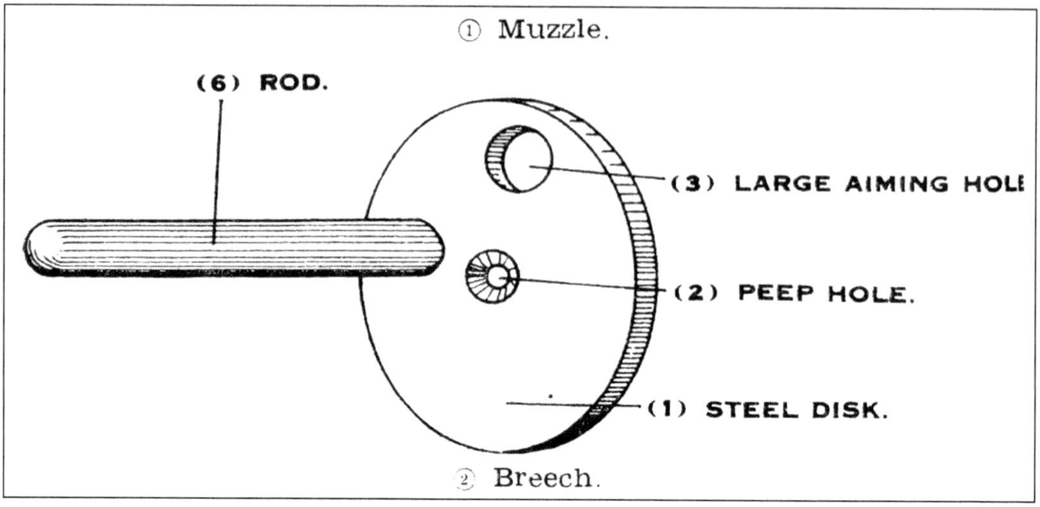

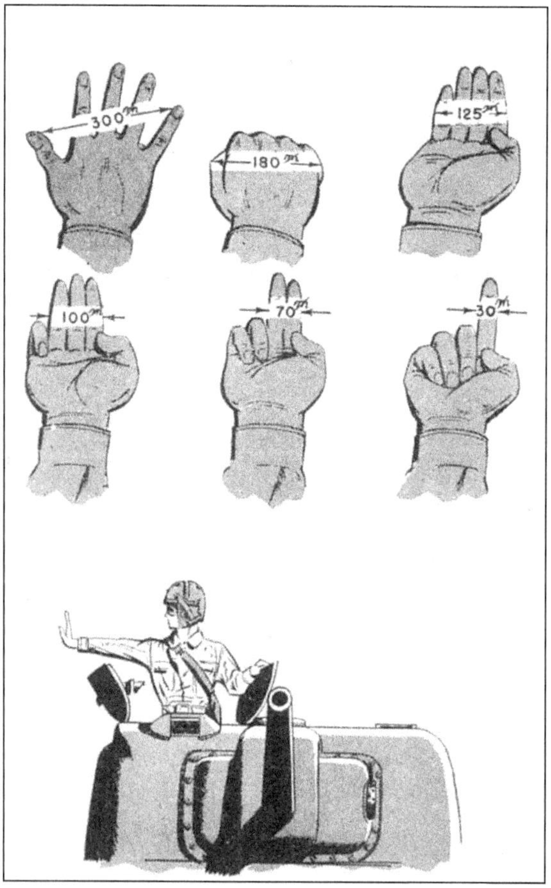

Above: Breech-end boresight. (FM 23-81, *Basic Field Manual 37-MM Gun, Tank M6 (Mounted in Tanks)*)

Left: Hand positions used to estimate angles in milliradians often referred to as mils. When this angle is coupled with the known length of a target vehicle, one can calculate the range and aim accordingly. The single finger is approximately 30 mils at arms' length. (FM 17-12, *Armored Force Field Manual, Tank Gunnery*)

Right: M6 periscope used on the driver's hatch, commander's hatch and gunner's hatch. (Roberts Collection)

Below: Practice tank course. (FM 17-15, *Armored Force Field Manual, Combat Practice Firing Armored Force Units*)

even training with radio communication failure was carried out using signal flags.

The drawing on the previous page depicts a practice tank course for enhancing crew coordination and skill level. Blank ammunition was authorized to add realism to the training. The tank commander directed the tank to the starting point. The tank started along the route and encountered a machine-gun position at position 1. The tank returned fire with its bow or coaxial machine gun and overran the position. The next challenge was at position 2, an anti-tank gun. The tank commander directed the tank to the cover behind a hill and then to rapidly attack and overwhelm the enemy crew. Traveling on to position 3, the tank was engaged by an anti-tank gun at position 4 and a machine gun at position 5. The tank commander took out the more formidable target leaving the machine gun for other tanks behind. The tank commander then observed a command post at position 6, attacked it and then performed reconnaissance on the vehicles and equipment at position 7. Traveling on to position 8, the tank fired on infantry in that area and proceeded to position 9, where the tank destroyed a mortar position. Moving on to position 10, the tank commander observed an enemy tank at position 11, engaged the tank and destroyed it. This competed the practice course and the tank proceeded to the finish for debriefing and critiquing.

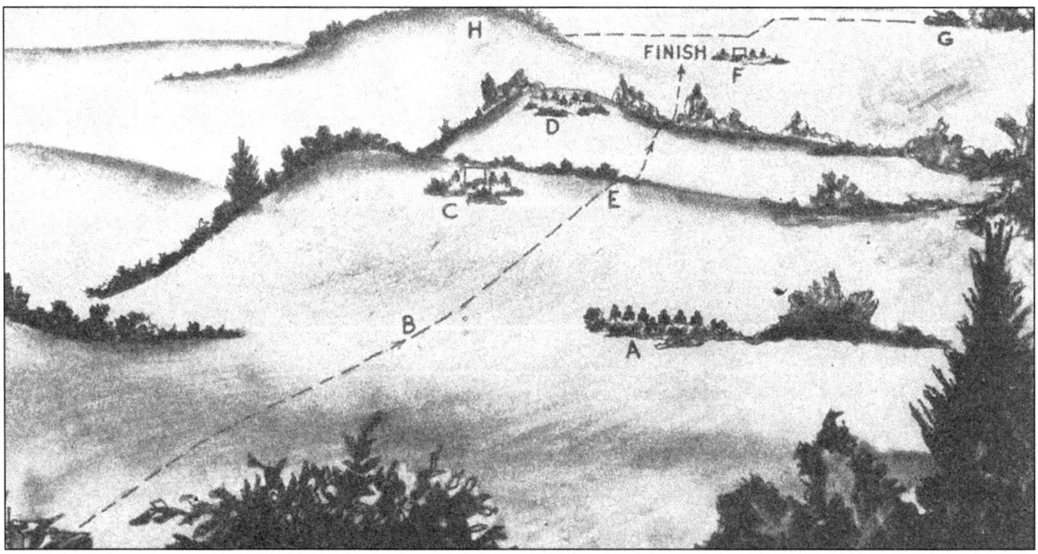

Live ammunition firing range. (FM 17-15, *Armored Force Field Manual, Combat Practice Firing Armored Force Units*)

The 151st used live ammunition in training. The drawing on the page opposite depicts a tank-training combat range where live ammunition was used. The tank moved along a route to position B taking fire from infantry at position A. A simulated machine gun at position C and infantry at position D were observed. The tank commander directed live fire at these positions using the main gun and onboard machine guns. The tank then traveled to position E and was engaged by an anti-tank gun at position F. The tank commander ordered the driver to place the tank in a defilade position and engaged the anti-tank gun. The tank then moved toward the finish line and engaged a tank at position G. The enemy tank then withdrew to position H behind a hill. After the engagement, the guns were cleared and the tank returned to the starting point for the debriefing. Live firing a machine gun at a tank with the crew inside might also have been part of the procedure depending on the availability of ammunition at that time. The target tank was stripped of fragile parts such as headlights, horn, tool kits and other sensitive items. The 0.30 cal. machine gun would be fired at the tank but would not penetrate the armor, giving confidence to those inside. It also gave the crew training on detecting where the source of the fire was located based on machine-gun projectile impacts with the tank.

The tank platoon (five-tank unit) combat range is shown on the next page. This course was designed to test the leadership of the platoon leader in maneuvering his unit through various obstacles and engaging various targets. Radio communication between tanks was very important in this exercise as it was essential for the platoon leader in

M22 tanks lined up in the motor pool. (Hughes, 'The 151st Airborne Tank Company')

Five-tank combat range. (FM 17-15, *Armored Force Field Manual, Combat Practice Firing Armored Force Units*)

maintaining control in fire and maneuver. The platoon leader issued orders and the tanks of the platoon maneuvered in concert with these orders. The platoon started at position A with the mission to take and hold position B. After emerging from the tree line, the platoon came under fire from an anti-tank gun at position C. The platoon leader maneuvered the platoon into cover and sent two tanks to the flank of the anti-tank gun. All tanks simultaneously engaged the anti-tank gun, destroyed it and regrouped to attack another anti-tank gun at position D. The platoon leader orders two tanks to position F and the rest of the tanks to position E to support the engagement of the lead tanks at D. With position D destroyed, the machine gun at position G was bypassed to engage the mission objective at B, which consisted of infantry and three machine-gun positions.

A competition between platoons could be held on a course like that depicted on the page opposite. This could develop rivalry between platoons, which contributed to sharpening crew skills.

The layout on p. 100 is a company level combat course. The company started at position A with the objective being position B. The company commander guided platoons to the objective, on the way encountering various obstacles, such as anti-tank guns, tanks and infantry.

On 30 January 1944, the Platoon Combat Tests were successfully completed by the 151st. During February, two new officers were assigned to the unit: Captain Felix D. Hege, the new company commander, who

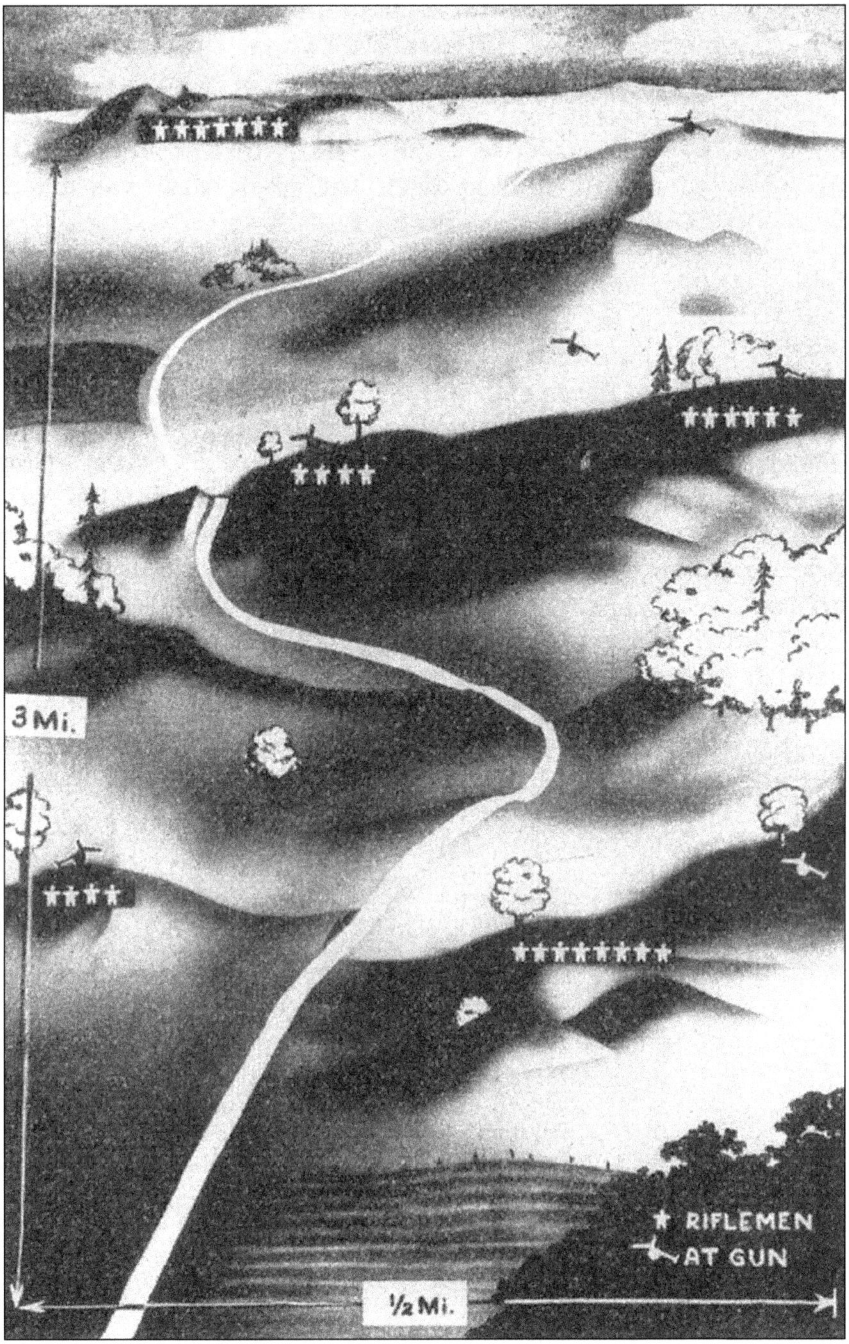

Platoon level test course. (FM 17-15, *Armored Force Field Manual, Combat Practice Firing Armored Force Units*)

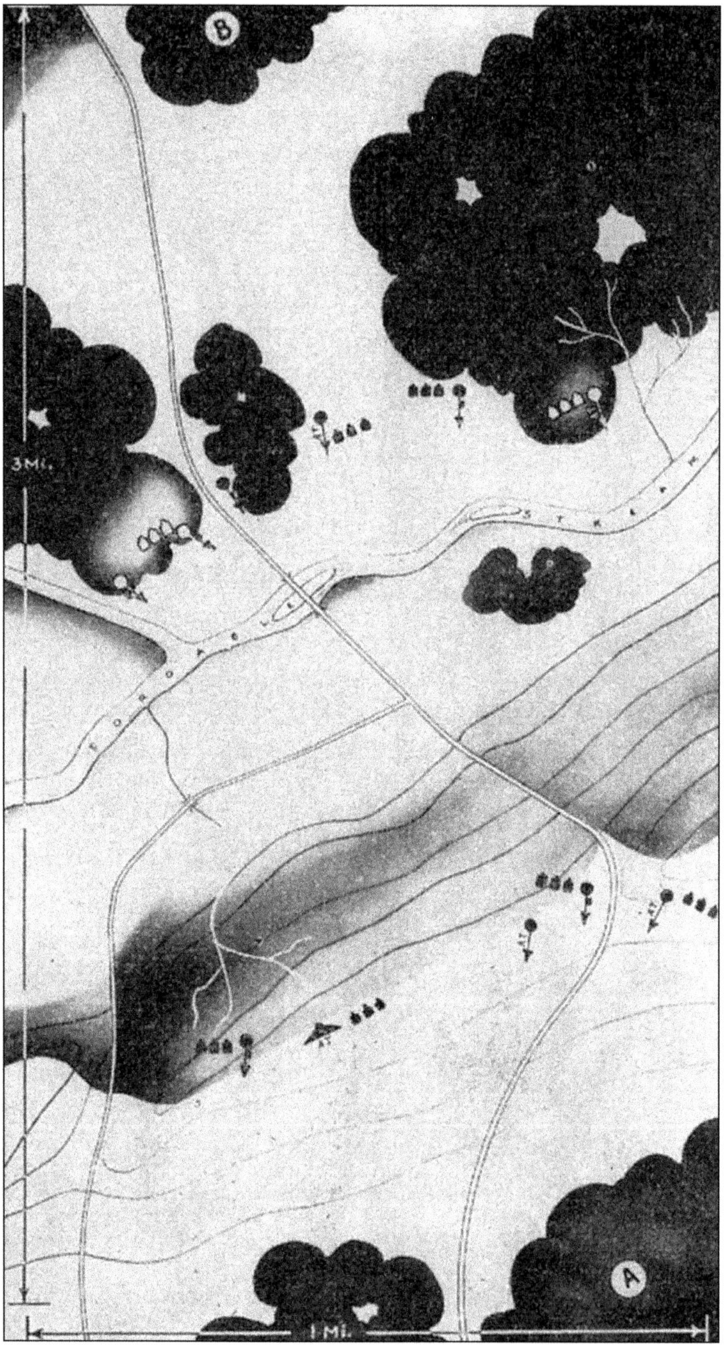

Company level test course. (FM 17-15, *Armored Force Field Manual, Combat Practice Firing Armored Force Units*)

came from the Armored Center, and 2nd Lieutenant George B. Busch, from the 28th Airborne Tank Battalion. Lieutenant Elvin Bass left the company for the 28th.

When 1st Sergeant Norton was sent to the ARTC, Fort Knox, Kentucky on 4 March 1944, Staff Sergeant Varney became the 1st Sergeant. In April, 1st Lieutenant Parson was transferred out. During May, the unit engaged in the combat intelligence test, the air-ground test and basic medical test. In July, the company moved from Fort Knox to Camp Mackall, North Carolina. The unit strength at this time was 6 officers and 129 enlisted men. The unit underwent glider training and became an airborne unit. On 29 August 1944, the company qualified as a glider-borne unit. During this period, 1st Lieutenant Gross left the company to become a paratrooper.

Right: A banner obtained by Lieutenant August Dreier at Camp Mackall. (Roberts Collection)

Below: A CG-10 glider, one of the candidates to deliver the M22. (National Archives)

CG-10 glider with flaps down in landing configuration. (David Wood Collection).

The Airborne Command struggled with developing a way to deliver the M22 to the battlefield. An early idea was to sling it to the fuselage of a C-54 and carry the turret in the aircraft. Initially, this was accomplished with four fittings, two on each side of the hull, to accept the hoist cables. This worked, but it was deemed unacceptable since the C-54 could only land on prepared, undamaged runways. This tended to defeat the purpose of the M22, which was to arrive at the battle line with the airborne troops.

Using the CG-10 glider was considered. The vehicle fit in its cargo bay, but its weight, approximately 16,400lb, was much more than the glider's maximum load capacity of 12,500lb. Lacking an effective delivery system, Airborne Command began to lose interest in the viability of the 151st Airborne Tank Company and 28th Airborne Tank Battalion.

In mid-1944, a joint staff composed of officers from the XXII Corps, the Airborne Center and the I Troop Carrier Command was formed to

A M22 hull secured to a C-54 with the turret inside the aircraft. (National Archives)

An M22 secured to the fuselage inside a CG-10 glider. (National Archives)

plan a large maneuver using airborne troops and ground forces. This was to be a combined Airborne-Troop Carrier maneuver conducted in the North Carolina maneuver area in the vicinity of Camp Mackall with a time frame of 24 September 1944. The purpose was two-fold. First, to aid in training Airborne and Troop Carrier staffs in the operation of airborne units. They were expected to experience planning, supervising and directing airborne operations. Second, Airborne and Troop Carrier units would experience air movement, rapid assembly and mock attack by combined forces both during the day and at night time.

The large-scale maneuver was planned to take place at Camp Mackall utilizing the 13th Airborne Division. The 151st Airborne Tank Company was slated to participate in this maneuver. This maneuver turned out to be the last large division-level maneuver and the largest night operation of the Second World War at the Airborne Center at Camp Mackall. It was to start in mid-July 1944, but the need for replacements for overseas units had resulted in a shortage of trained personnel that delayed the start of the maneuver. In September, units of the 13th Airborne Division moved from Camp Mackall to staging areas at Lumberton Auxilliary Airfield. The maneuver started on 24 September, having been postponed a day because of poor weather conditions. The initial objective was to capture the airport at Camp Mackall. The plan for aircraft was that after taking off, they would fly a serpentine route to simulate the typical flying time to an objective.

The following list details the units involved in the maneuver:

Blue Force	**Red Force**	**Task Force**
13th Airborne Division	151st Airborne Tank Bn	Staffs of Airborne Command,
60th Troop Carrier Wing	89th Division Recon. Troop	Troop Carrier Command,
Units I Tactical Air	841st Anti-Aircraft Art. Bn	XXII Corps
Division	161st Airborne Engineer Bn	4105 Quarter Master Co. (truck)
130th Evacuation Hospital		4107 Quarter Master Co. (truck)
		3978 Quarter Master Co. (truck)
		85th Signal Operations Co.
		Provost Marshall MP Co.
		511 Medical Collection Co.
		512 Medical Collection Co.

The Task Force directed the maneuver and provided various services required for the operation. The Blue Force was to conduct an airborne operation and attack positions defended by the Red Force, a ground force defending positions throughout the maneuver area. The Red Force was ordered to simulate German forces throughout all phases of the maneuver, and each unit of Red Force was to conform to an actual German unit. Some units were actual US Army units with names changed to represent German units. Other units were simulated because of a shortage of personnel.

The order of battle for the Red Force was as follows:

A. Ground force

XXXIV Armeekorps (Infantry Corps)
384th Infanteriedivision (Simulated)
376th Infanteriedivision (Simulated)
212th Infanteriedivision (Simulated)
316th Grenadierregiment (Infantry Regiment represented by the 161st Airborne Engineer Battalion)
320th Grenadierregiment (Simulated)
423rd Grenadierregiment (Simulated)
212th Artillerieregiment (One battalion represented by liaison officer and fire markers)
212th Schiele Abteilung (Mobile battalion represented by a company from the reconnaissance troop of the 89th Infantry Division)
841st Leichte Flakabteilung (Light anti-aircraft battalion represented by the 841st anti-aircraft artillery battalion)
151st Panzer Abteilung (Tank battalion represented by the 151st Airborne Tank Company)
221st Landesschutzenbataillon (Local defense battalion represented by 161st Airborne Engineer Battalion)

B. Air Forces
26th Jagdgeschwader (Single-engine fighter group – simulated)
11th Nahaufklarungsgruppen (Short-range reconnaissance squadron – simulated)

Since the 151st Airborne Tank Company did not have a means of delivering the tanks by air, the unit was relegated to acting as a German tank battalion and did not benefit from the airborne nature of the maneuver. Paratroopers of the 515th Parachute Infantry Regiment jumped at three drop zones at night in high wind conditions. This, coupled with aircraft not unloading at the proper point, resulted in paratroopers scattered over the area, a typical problem encountered in combat jumps, as evidenced in Operation Overlord. The paratroopers were able to rapidly assemble, attack and capture the airfield. As morning dawned, reinforcements came in by glider transport with C47s towing two CG-4 gliders or one CG-13 glider. Approximately 200 CG-4A troops arrived by C47s and B-17s which could then land on the captured airfield. (It should be noted that although the B-17s were bombers and not troop carriers, they were probably used because of a shortage of C47s.) Engineer battalions built bridges for troop movement around swamps and barriers to aid in fortifying the newly won positions. On 25 September 1944, the airborne phase ended and the ground phases began. Apparently, as was typical of maneuvers at that time, health-related problems concerning hygiene, such as dysentery, trench mouth, etc., developed rapidly, according to records from the 22nd Medical Company. There was an isolated battalion that was supplied by air for three days. One result of such a large airborne operation was the recommendation that gliders land at dawn for better visibility unless night landing was absolutely necessary. By noon, Blue Force had attacked and captured a 120 square mile area held by Red Force, of which the 151st was a member. Fighter planes and A-20 attack bombers supported the assault.

This was the largest night parachute jump in the country, with over 2,000 paratroopers jumping and over 10,000 soldiers landing in aircraft. This was the first time the CG-13 glider was used in an operation. Areas blacked out during the maneuver were parts of Moore, Scotland and Hoke Counties. Hoffman and Derby sections were also blacked out. The 13th Airborne Division had already given up many of its best-trained paratroopers to the Pacific and European theaters in April and May of 1944. Many had participated in Operation Overlord and Operation Dragoon. Most of those transferring from the 13th Airborne Division went to the 82nd and 101st Airborne Divisions. In late January 1945, the 13th Airborne Division left Camp Mackall for Camp Shanks, New York in preparation for movement overseas.

During the maneuvers from 24 September–6 October 1944, the 151st took part as an enemy force at Camp Mackall and was awarded a satisfactory rating during the maneuvers. While portraying an enemy tank unit, the tankers had to follow specific orders and scripts to make the maneuver work. After the maneuver, a detachment of men from the 151st was sent to Washington, DC to take part in an airborne demonstration at the end of October 1944. Physical fitness tests and

The airport at Camp Mackall, which was the initial objective of the 13th Airborne Division during the maneuver. (US Army Report)

Gliders landing at glider landing zone number 3. (US Army Report)

B-17 bombers used to deliver troops to the captured airfield. (US Army Report)

Troops moving up toward positions defended by the 151st Airborne Tank Company. (US Army Report)

From left to right: General Henry Terrell, Jr, General Eldridge Chapman and Colonel Pitts. General Terrell was the commander XXII Corps and the 13th Airborne was part of this corps. General Chapman was the commander of the 13th Airborne Division. Colonel Pitts was on the staff of the Sixteenth Troop Carrier Wing Army Air Forces. (US Army Report)

Colonel Dalbey, second from the left, was commander of the US Army Airborne Center Camp Mackall, North Carolina, the organization that hosted the maneuvers. He is seen here with distinguished visitors. (US Army Report)

Individual Proficiency Tests were passed by all members of the unit in November. The rating of the unit was 96.1 for the physical fitness test. Tank-crew gunnery classes were completed in December 1944 with most receiving a First Class gunner's rating. With Allied advancements in Europe, there was an urgent need for trained personnel as replacements. Airborne Command saw no further use for the 151st, mainly because of a lack of a vehicle delivery system. Consequently, Headquarters Airborne Center GO #15, dated 20 December 1944 inactivated the 151st Airborne Tank Company effective 31 December 1944. The officers were assigned to the Armor Replacement Pool at Fort Knox, Kentucky. The enlisted men were disbursed among armored units throughout the United States. The same fate was experienced by the 28th Airborne Tank Battalion, which was inactivated at approximately the same time. Some of the M22 Locust tanks were sent to England, the rest remained in the United States for training purposes.

The photo on the page opposite shows an M22 at the dirt track at Aberdeen Proving Grounds on 29 August 1944 with clods of dirt flying around. By mid-1944, the US Army considered the M22 obsolete and designated it a limited standard. The plan was to use the tank for training and send a number of them to the British under Lend Lease.

An M22 airborne tank being used in training at Aberdeen Proving Grounds, Maryland, 1944. (US Army Signal Corps)

A T-9E1, eventually designated M22, at Aberdeen Proving Grounds, Maryland, 29 August 1944. (Roberts Collection)

The caption below tells a slightly different story. The sentence, 'This tank is proving its worth on invasion fronts the world over.' is incorrect. The tank had not been used in any invasion anywhere in the world at that time; an example of propaganda of the time, a 'slight' exaggeration.

FOR RELEASE: MONDAY, SEPTEMBER 4, 1944.

735741. . . . . .NEW YORK BUREAU

AIRBORNE TANK GOES THROUGH MANEUVERS

ABERDEEN, MD. -- THE T9E1, A NEW AIRBORNE TANK, BOUNCES OVER THE OBSTACLE COURSE AT ABERDEEN PROVING GROUND DURING A DEMONSTRATION FOR THE PRESS ON AUGUST 29, 1944. THIS TANK IS PROVING ITS WORTH ON INVASION FRONTS THE WORLD OVER.

BU

CREDIT (ACME) 9/1/44 (MD)

FOR RELEASE: MONDAY, SEPTEMBER 4, 1944.

The official caption for the photograph above. (Roberts Collection)

Chapter 4

US Airborne Tank Usage in the Second World War

The major impediment to airborne tank usage, according to the US Army, was transporting the M22 tank to the battlefield. It took about 30 minutes to unload the tank and put the turret on for battle. The British thought this to be too long since a few minutes as a sitting duck on the battlefield could be decisive. Additionally, serviceable airfields were not guaranteed behind enemy lines, and the M22 tank was becoming

A Locust unloading from a Hamilcar glider in England. Note the short gun tube which was set up to fit the Littlejohn adapter which added length to the gun tube. (Wikimedia Commons)

obsolete. The armor of the M22 was too thin (could not stop 0.50 cal. armor-piercing ammunition), the 37mm gun was ineffective against most German frontal armor, and other mechanical problems remained unsolved. The T-9 was redesignated the M22 light tank and classified a limited standard in September 1944, not to be used by the US military in combat. It was relegated to units as a training vehicle.

The British, however, maintained an interest in the T-9 as a replacement for the Tetrarch since it would fit in a Hamilcar glider. A T-9E1 prototype flew in a Hamilcar in July 1943, verifying the viability of delivering it behind enemy lines. Hamilcar production was behind schedule and the newer light versions of the T-9E1 Locust had to be tested. Testing by the British showed several deficiencies in the operation of the tank and the use of its main gun. Despite this, the British declared the vehicle operational and ready for combat. Locust light tanks were delivered to the Airborne Light Tank Squadron in October 1943. Approximately 260 tanks were given to the British under the Lend Lease Act of 1941.

In September 1943, Littlejohn adapters arrived for evaluation. This was a squeeze-bore adapter that was connected to the muzzle of the 37mm main gun. A tungsten carbide cartridge was used. When the cartridge was fired, the soft metal of the outer casing of the 37mm projectile was squeezed down to 30mm, which significantly increased the velocity and armor penetrating capability of the shot. The kinetic round achieved a velocity of approximately 4,000ft per second. The velocity of a standard 37mm round was approximately 3,000ft per second. The gun tube was shortened to receive the adapter.

In October 1943, the British 6th Airborne received seventeen Locust T-9 light tanks that were then sent to Warcop ranges in Westmorland, England the following month to fire 37mm high-explosive rounds at practice targets in November 1943. At the end of 1943, the 6th Airborne Armored Reconnaissance Regiment had seventeen Locust light tanks equipped with the 37mm main gun and sixteen Tetrarch light tanks equipped with the 2-pounder main gun. As Operation Overlord approached, Hamilcar gliders were being prepared for the invasion. In March 1944, twenty-three Hamilcar gliders were reserved to carry seventeen T-9 Locust tanks; the other six gliders were held in reserve as replacements.

There was uncertainty about which tank to use in glider operations. The Locust suffered from mechanical problems while the Tetrarch was considered obsolete compared with the newer Locust. A last-minute decision was made to keep the T-9 Locust tanks in reserve, and Tetrarch tanks were used at D-Day.

A Locust from the 6th Airborne Reconnaissance Regiment exiting a Hamilcar. (Roberts Collection)

An M22 locust and tank-crew member in 6th Airborne Reconnaissance Regiment uniform, (reenacted). Notice the Pegasus symbol on the left front side of the vehicle, the emblem of the 6th Reconnaissance Regiment. (Roberts Collection)

A Locust equipped with the Littlejohn adapter. (Roberts Collection)

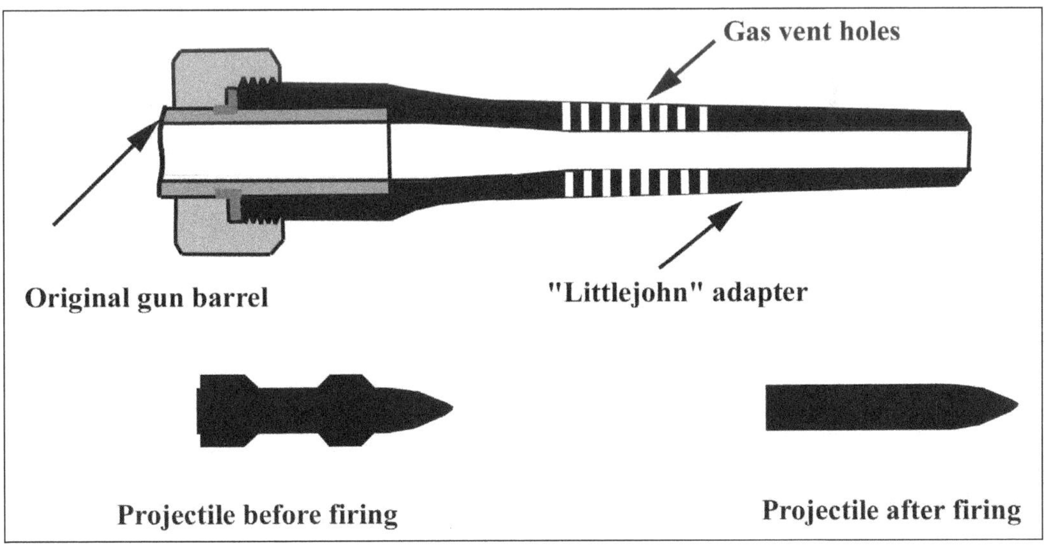

Little John adapter and projectiles before and after firing.

Hamilcar glider production by the British was slow as a result of wood shortages and management difficulties. The relatively limited number of these gliders meant that they would only be available to the British airborne forces. After a glider was manufactured, it was towed to RAF North Luffenham in Rutland to have its specific cargo loaded. It should be noted that ballast had to be added to tow the glider if no cargo was onboard, in order to maintain the proper balance point specified for the aircraft. After loading cargo, the glider was flown to RAF Tarrant Rushton for training and preparation for an assault. Training between 1943 and 1944 included take-offs and landings with an instructor and then solo flights. Typically, the tank crews were in the vehicles that were carried by the gliders at the time of training. Procedures for utilizing tanks in airborne operation were developed during training.

Before a glider carrying a tank was released from the tug aircraft, the tank engine was started and warmed up. There was an exhaust hose that would allow the exhaust to exit the glider. The typical carburetor engines of the time were often hard to start and did not operate well when cold, causing them to stall when a load was applied to the engine. Obviously, it would be detrimental if the glider had landed and the tank stalled upon exiting the glider, as often these engines were difficult to restart after a stall.

Consequently, engine warm-up prior to landing was a necessity. The Locust fit tightly inside the glider so crews often would stay in the vehicle prior to landing. This also allowed a measure of protection from small-arms fire. After landing, the driver pulled on a rope that released the tank from its tie downs and opened the front clam-shell door, allowing the tank to exit the aircraft quickly. If the door failed to open, it was still possible for the tank to drive through the wood / fabric doors and exit the glider, and this did happen.

By March 1945, the Allies had reached the Rhine River at several locations as a result of the wide-front doctrine championed by General Eisenhower, who planned to eliminate all enemy resistance east of the Rhine in preparation for the final drive into Germany. The XXX Corps pushed the Germans from their final positions west of the Rhine at the town of Wesel with great difficulty. Operation Plunder, to be led by Field Marshall Montgomery, was to be the amphibious crossing of the Rhine on 23 March 1945. Operation Varsity was to be the airborne assault in support of Operation Plunder. The first usage of the M22 Locust airborne tank occurred during Operation Varsity. Operations Plunder and Varsity were to be the first significant crossing of the Rhine.

Unexpectedly on 7 March 1945, the Ludendorff bridge at Remagen was captured and Allied units poured across until 25 March when the

Locust tie down in a Hamilcar glider, a very tight fit. (http: / / www.historyofwar.org / Pictures / pictures_m22_locust_hamilcar.html)

bridge suddenly collapsed. Operation Varsity, the airborne assault to secure a foothold on the east bank of the Rhine, was to be carried out by XVIII Corps, composed of the US 17th Airborne Division and the British 6th Airborne Division, under the command of Major General Matthew Ridgeway with British Major General Gale as second in command. Ridgeway's orders, received on 27 February 1945, were to conduct an airborne assault in the vicinity of Wesel and thwart enemy attacks against Allied forces crossing the Rhine.

The area to be secured by the airborne forces was Diersfordter Wald, a highland forest northwest of Wesel. There were several farm fields in the area that were suitable for glider landing operations. This area overlooked the Rhine River crossing to be used by the British 12th Corps. The British 6th Airborne Division was tasked with securing the high ground north of Bergen, and with capturing the town of Hamminkeln and bridges over the Ussel River in that area. The British were to hold this area until relieved by the ground force that had crossed the

Rhine in the amphibious landing. Eight Hamilcars of the 6th Airborne Armored Reconnaissance Regiment transported M22 Locust light tanks. The 17th Airborne Division was assigned the southern half of the Diersfordter Wald, while the northern half was assigned to the 6th Airborne Division. Operation Varsity benefitted from the experiences of Operation Overlord and Operation Market Garden.

The line of assault of the ground forces would be close to that of the airborne drop zones so that the link-up could occur on the first day. The airborne assault would take place during daylight hours to ensure maximum visibility for glider landings. This proved to be problematic in that German anti-aircraft gunners would have a good view of the large, slow-moving Hamilcar gliders, making targeting much easier than at night. Allied aerial superiority made daylight operations practical. The airborne objectives were within range of artillery should additional firepower be required. Consequently, the entire airborne operation would occur in one drop. Six drop and landing zones were selected. The drop zones were designated 'A', and 'B'; the landing zones 'P', 'R', 'O' and 'U'. The amphibious crossing of the Rhine was to start at 2200 hours on 23 March 1945. The airborne assault was set to start at 1000 hours the following morning. The force opposing the drops and landings was the German 84th ID part of the 6th Corps. The Germans, expecting an airborne assault, had stationed several anti-aircraft batteries in the vicinity of the drop and landing zones.

Operation Varsity (crossing the Rhine) was the largest single airborne assault in history with more than 21,000 troops using over 1,500 aircraft and over 1,300 gliders. This force was far superior to the German Army defending the area. The 6th Airborne Armored Regiment with the Locust tanks was to be transported by Group 38 using the Hamilcar gliders and Halifax four-engine bombers as the towing aircraft. The whole operation severely taxed Allied resources and personnel. A shortage of glider pilots, a result of casualties from Market Garden, required transferring pilots from powered aircraft squadrons, and several crews had not entirely completed their training. Powered-aircraft pilots had to undergo glider pilot training and combat soldier training as they were expected to fight as soldiers after their gliders had landed. The paratroopers were scheduled to jump first, followed by the glider landings. Two paratroop brigades dropped first to secure Diersfordter Wald; 6th Airborne Division Headquarters and the eight Locust tanks in Hamilcar gliders would land at landing zone 'P' with divisional troops. All forty-eight

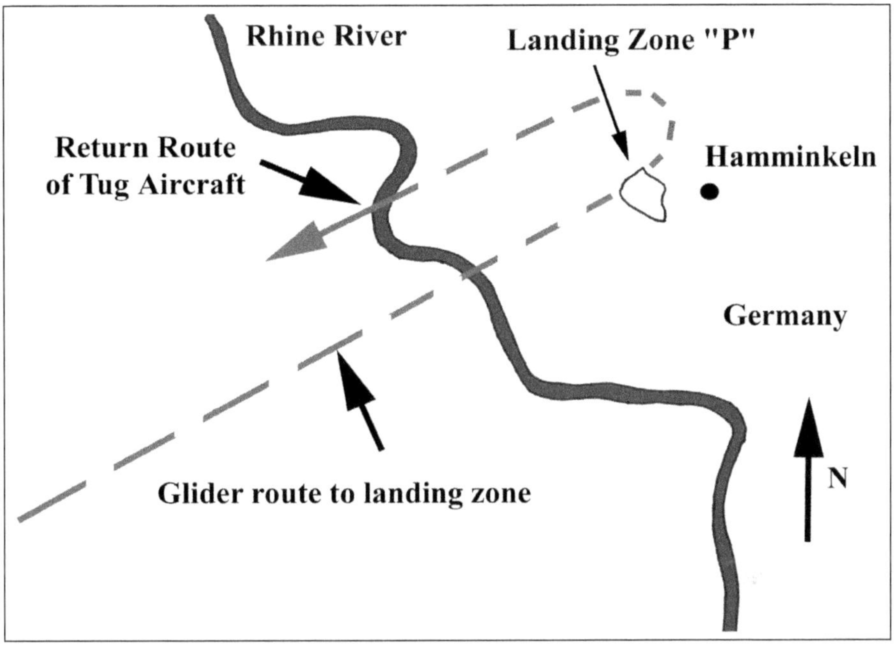

The glider route from England to landing zone 'P' for the 8 Locust airborne tanks. As the gliders crossed the Rhine, they encountered heavy anti-aircraft fire with several Hamilcars being hit. After release over the landing zone, the tug aircraft performed a 180-degree turn for the return route.

Hamilcars took off from Woodbridge in Suffolk, England, with eight carrying the Locust tanks. The payload of the remaining Hamilcars were carriers, artillery, supplies and troops.

Lieutenant Colonel Stewart was the commander of the small squadron of eight tanks. The headquarters squadron consisted of two tanks, and the two troops contained three tanks each. Upon landing, the tanks were directed to group at the southwestern edge of landing zone 'P'. The tanks were then to move to defend the high ground on the eastern edges of Diersfordter Wald.

The crews for the squadron of eight tanks were three officers and twenty-four enlisted men. From 17–20 March 1945, tanks were loaded at Tarrant Rushton and gliders towed to Woodbridge on 20 and 21 March. Tank engines were run periodically to assess readiness for the airborne assault. Battle briefings occurred on 22 and 23 March. At 0720 hours on 24 March, the gliders were towed into the air and arrived above the landing zones without incident, under good weather conditions. On its approach to the landing zone, the Hamilcar glider code-named

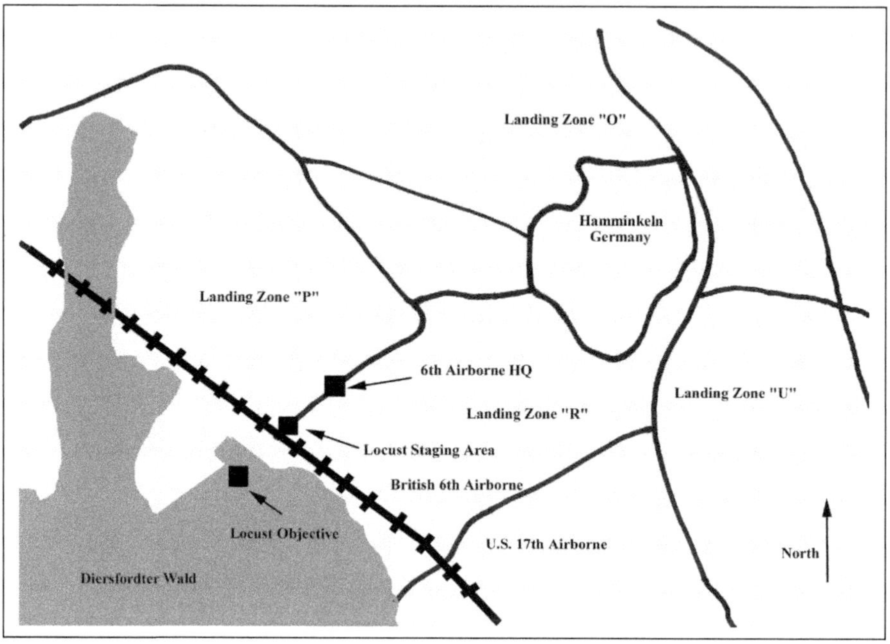

A map showing the situation on 24 March 1945.

Lieutenant Kenward's Locust before being knocked out by the 88 from a self-propelled gun. The damage to the right rear sand skirt matches that in the next photograph. The damage was probably caused by punching through the jammed cargo door of the Hamilcar where some piece of structure from the glider got caught in the rear idler wheel. (http://commons.wikimedia.org/wiki/Commons)

Lieutenant Kenward's Locust was knocked out close to a Hamilcar glider seen in the background. The gunner's hatch cover is resting on the front glacis plate. This tank was supporting American infantry in an attack at a farm when it was knocked out by a German armored vehicle. The hit was at the left rear, which is probably why the gunner was killed. The commander-loader survived, along with the driver. (Imperial War Museum, Cambridge, UK)

'Chalk 262' carrying the Locust commanded by Sergeant Dawson, suffered a midair structural failure that caused the tank to fall through the floor of the glider. The bodies of the crew were found several months later at the edge of the Rhine. The glider was piloted by Lieutenant Graefe and Sergeant James and towed by a Halifax bomber of the 298th squadron. As they approached the landing zone, the seven remaining Hamilcars with their Locusts encountered fire from German FLAK batteries and reduced visibility from Allied artillery fire and air-attack smoke. Although air and artillery attacks were supposed to suppress the FLAK batteries, some survived, and the large, slow-moving gliders were easy targets. The smoke made it difficult to recognize the expected landing zone and to estimate the height and approach speed. The Commanding Officer's glider landed successfully despite FLAK damage to its wheels. Lieutenant Davies and his Locust also made a successful landing despite FLAK damage. The glider containing Lieutenant Kenward's tank landed successfully, but hard, jamming the front doors of the glider. Lieutenant Kenward, realizing the problem, ordered Sergeant Colin Peckham, the tank's driver, to drive through the glider door, which was made of wood and fabric. The tank exited the glider unscathed but shortly afterward encountered a German armored vehicle with large-caliber gun. Later accounts of what followed vary.

Stephen Wright described the armored vehicle that fired on Lieutenant Kenward's tank as a Panther tank firing an 88mm projectile.*

Keith Flint described it as a self-propelled gun firing an 88mm projectile.** Tim Saunders simply described the projectile as an 88.*** Based on these descriptions, the most likely German armored vehicle encountered by Lieutenant Kenward's Locust was either a Jagdpanther self-propelled gun or a Panzerkampfwagen V Panther, vehicles that look similar at first glance. The Panther had a turret and a 75mm high-velocity gun, the projectile of which was easily confused with that of an 88. Both vehicles had similar side-armor configuration. Several 37mm rounds were fired at the German armored vehicle by Kenward, with no effect. The German armored vehicle knocked out the Locust with a single shot, killing one crewman, the gunner in the turret. Lieutenant Kenward was wounded in the thigh and Sergeant Peckham was burned on the left leg. American medics treated the survivors, who were then evacuated by a DUKW (amphibious troop carrier).

Analyzing this engagement is difficult without more detailed accounts from the participants. However, some conclusions can be reached. Firing several rounds at the German armored vehicle required the Locust to remain nearly stationary since it did not have a gun tube

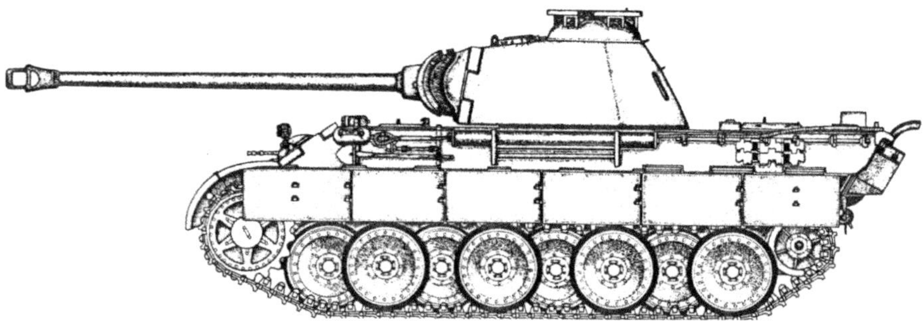

Panzerkampfwagen V Panther.

* Stephen Wright, *The Last Drop, Operation Varsity March 24–25, 1945*, Stackpole, 2008.

** Keith Flint, *Airborne Armour*, Helion and Company Limited, 2004.

*** Tim Saunders, *Operation Varsity, the British and Canadian Airborne Assault*, Pen & Sword Military, 2008.

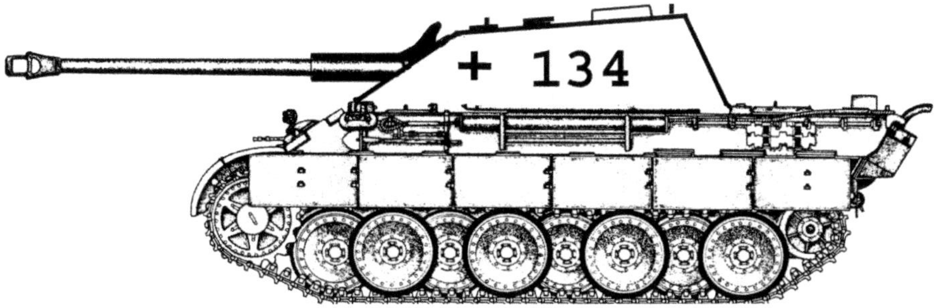

Jagdpanther Sd.Kfz. 173.

leveler. The hit at the rear of the Locust suggests that it was at an angle to the German armored vehicle when hit, based on the damage to the left side of the vehicle seen in the photo of Lieutenant Kenward's knocked-out tank on p. 121. The gun tube is angled to the left presumably aiming at the target, also suggesting that the hull of the Locust was at an angle to the German vehicle.

The frontal armor of a Panther or a Jagdpanther is impervious to the standard 37mm projectile, but vulnerable to the Littlejohn projectile at about 100yd. Lieutenant Kenward's tank did not have the Littlejohn adapter. The 37mm Gun M6 with Littlejohn adapter had the following penetration in rolled homogeneous steel armor at 30-degree obliquity:*

Range in Yards	Penetration in Inches
109	4.64
546	3.35
1090	2.32
1640	1.81

The Jagdpanther had sloped frontal armor of approximately 3.14in which made the vehicle nearly invulnerable to fire from the M22 Locust using the standard 37mm M51 projectile. While the frontal armor of the Panther was similar, its side armor was thin, 1.6 to 2in, and was not significantly sloped. This made it vulnerable to standard 37mm projectiles. The following pages show armor penetration capability of the 37mm projectile. It could be argued that Lieutenant

* *Fire and Movement*, The Tank Museum at Bovington, Dorset, UK, 1975.

Kenward was attempting to maneuver the Locust to a position to attack the side armor of the Panther before his tank was hit. The right track was broken and is ahead of the tank, suggesting that the tank was moving forward when hit. Typically, a German gunner would aim at the center of mass of the target, but due to the forward movement of the Locust, the hit was to the rear of the center of mass. It was a common tactic for Allied tank crews to attack a Panther or Jagdpanther from the side. Panther and Jagdpanther crews would try to position their frontal armor facing enemy tanks because the side armor was vulnerable. Several 37mm-projectile strikes to the side armor of the Panther probably would have defeated it.

Three other Hamilcars crashed and one other landed successfully, but its Locust was damaged. One Hamilcar smashed through a house on landing, damaging the 37mm main gun on the Locust, but the machine gun was operable and supported members of the American

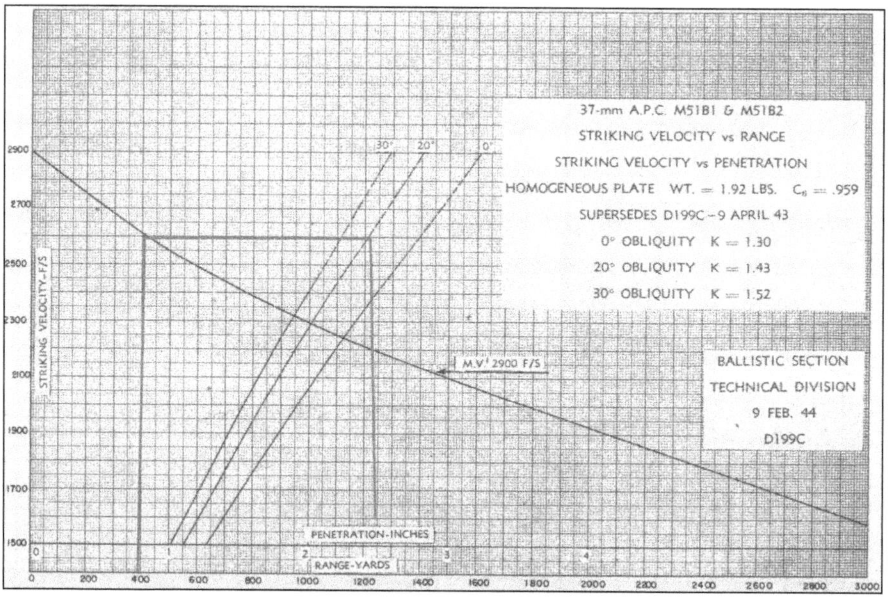

Terminal ballistic data for 37mm A.P.C. M51B1 armor piercing projectile for homogeneous steel plate. As an example: What is the range required to get a 2.5in penetration of homogeneous steel plate at 20-degree obliquity? As shown above, a 2.5in penetration is selected. Draw a vertical line to the 20-degree obliquity of the armor plate. Then draw a horizontal line to the left to the mean velocity curve. Then draw a vertical line downward to obtain the maximum range of 400yd in order to achieve a 2.5in penetration. (TM9-1907, *Ballistic Data Performance of Ammunition*)

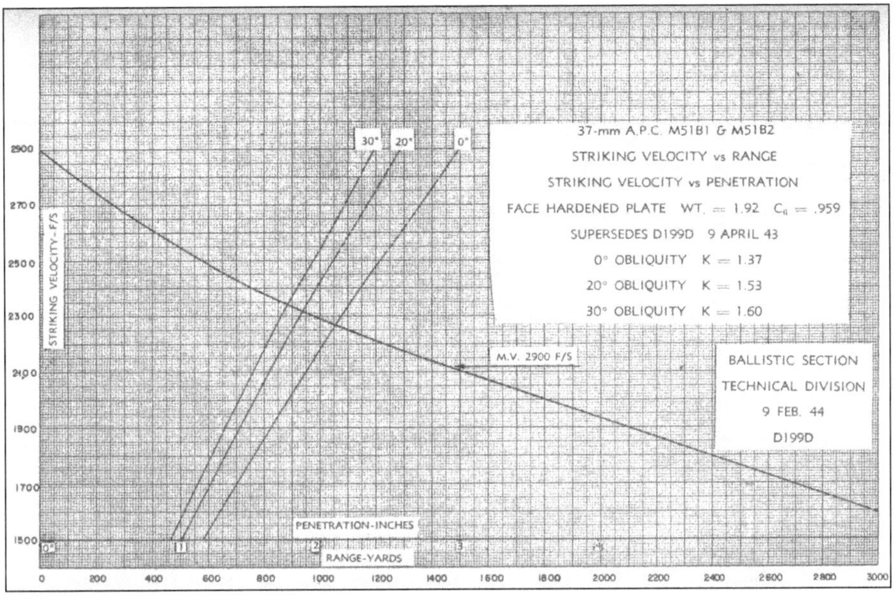

Terminal ballistic data for 37mm A.P.C. M51B1 armor piercing projectile for face hardened plate. (TM9-1907, *Ballistic Data Performance of Ammunition*)

513 PIR of the 17th Airborne Division who had been dropped at the wrong drop zone. Another glider nosed into a ditch upon landing, the impact causing the Locust it was carrying to be thrown free of the glider, landing upside down and out of action. Tanker K.W. Dowett was about to land when a FLAK gun shot off part of the glider's wing that was carrying his tank. The loss of control resulted in a severe crash that killed both glider pilots and left the tankers hanging upside down from their safety harnesses in the tank. Though shaken, the crew inside the tank got out and hitched a ride on the Commanding Officer Lieutenant Colonel Godfrey Stewart's tank that had landed successfully. The tank commanded by Corporal Ward arrived safely north of the landing zone but broke down while recovering a jeep from a Horsa glider. Ward's tank was then used as a stationary pillbox just ahead of the 12th Parachute Battalion. The tank used its 37mm gun and machine gun to support the Allied troop advance and ended up killing over 100 German soldiers.[21]

Before landing, Staff Sergeant Harry Dent and Staff Sergeant Dereck Rodgers were piloting their Hamilcar when the Halifax tug and glider ran into heavy flak. The tug was hit and engulfed in flames. Seeing this, the Hamilcar pilots released the tow rope and were able to land despite damage to the rudder and having had to release early. The Locust and tank crew were able to exit the glider and reach the rendezvous area, but both pilots were later taken prisoner.

The four surviving tanks occupied the high ground near the objective. Infantry reinforced by glider pilots were assigned to support the tanks. After the operation settled down and stabilized, four Locust tanks made it to their objective, with one having both an unserviceable main gun and radio and another with both an unserviceable machine gun and radio. This left two Locusts fully operational of the eight that set out for the invasion. It should be noted that other Hamilcars carrying heavy loads suffered a similar casualty rate.

Lieutenant Colonel Godfrey Stewart, having sent two Locusts to secure the high ground to hold off an enemy counter-attack, set up his command post and established communications with division headquarters. The other two tanks were held in reserve to cover the advance of the tanks at the high ground. The two tanks on the high ground engaged an enemy force, and infantry was brought up for support. A stalemate developed with the opposing German forces, who were knocking out tank periscopes with accurate rifle fire. Fire from a German infantry gun caused the two lead tanks to back off slightly, but the two tanks in the

A Halifax bomber towing a Hamilcar glider. This was the most successful means of delivering a tank to a battlefield in the Second World War. (IBCC Digital Archive)

The driver's vision periscope that is deployed when going into battle. German snipers were aiming to knock out these periscopes. There are a few spares that can be slid back into position but after several are damaged, the driver is nearly blind and so are the commander loader and/or gunner. (Roberts Collection)

rear were brought up to form a fortified line with help from glider pilots turned into infantry. The position was held until the next day when supporting forces arrived in the form of DD Sherman tanks and tank destroyers from the 44th Royal Tank Regiment. This link-up with the medium tanks completed the mission of the Locust light tanks.

Forty-eight Hamilcars took off from Woodridge successfully. About thirty-eight Hamilcars landed generically at the landing zones; some at the wrong landing zone or outside the landing zone.

The ten that did not make it were most likely victims of towing problems, anti-aircraft fire or structural failure. This was the largest flight of Hamilcars in the war to date.

Some problems with the Hamilcars while landing were observed. The fuselage had a tendency to get stuck in a ditch or depression and pitch over, making it difficult or impossible to unload. Lieutenant Colonel Stewart recommended skids be used, which were closer to the fuselage and would reduce the tendency to pitch over. He also drew attention to the need for a means of retracting the landing gear from the cockpit once the glider had landed to facilitate unloading and reduce vulnerability of the pilots to fire as they jacked down the landing gear in the cargo compartment. Finally, he recommended that the main gun of the Locusts be pointed to the rear to reduce the possibility of damage when landing since at least two Locusts had this problem during Operation Varsity. The gun tube on the Locust was short enough to traverse to the rear in the fuselage of the Hamilcar. The gun tube of the Tetrarch was too long and was blocked from traversing by the sidewalls of the fuselage. Despite all of this, the operation was considered a success as all objectives were achieved.

George Moodie of the 6th Airborne Armored Recce Regiment RAC is in the driver's seat of a M22 Locust light tank in Germany. Note that the lifting lugs have been removed, the headlight guards have been removed, the right sand skirt has broken off, with the remains at the rear of the vehicle, the right front fender is missing and the tracks are clean indicating that it has been running on paved surfaces. There is damage to the right rear fender, which apparently was common if something became engaged in the track and rotated upward near the idler wheel. The removal of the hardware was probably done to save weight. This is a rare photograph of one of the Locusts that survived Operation Varsity. (Roberts Collection)

The Locust light tanks were vulnerable to air attack and glider crashes, which limited the number available for action. However, the ones that were operational kept enemy forces busy and away from the headquarters location. There was criticism of the 37mm main gun as being ineffective. Certainly, the usage of the Littlejohn device and canister shot would have increased the lethality of the tank. The superiority of the Operation Varsity assault force overwhelmed the German forces in the area, resulting in the surrender or withdrawal of enemy soldiers. The Ruhr was overrun by the Allies by mid-April 1945, with over 300,000 German soldiers surrendering. Many German soldiers felt it was better to surrender to the American and British forces than to the Russians, so as they surrendered they would often march back to a prisoner collection area without a large escort. The Wehrmacht was a spent force, its command structure falling apart. What resistance remained came from small units whose effectiveness depended on their leadership, experience (volksstrum) or fanaticism (SS) leading to the surrender on 7 May 1945.

All Locust tanks sent to Europe were left there after the war. The Locust made its way to Belgium in 1946, and some fifty were in

This Egyptian M22 Locust was knocked out in the 1948 Arab-Israeli war during Operation Assaf. (Israel Defense Force, State of Israel)

M22 tanks in the United States were declared obsolete at the end of the Second World War and sold to farmers for plowing and other agricultural purposes. (US Army Signal Corps)

Above and opposite above: Locust, serial number 110, is seen before restoration, having been found abandoned in a farm field in the Midwest of the United States. (Roberts Collection)

M22 tanks at a salvage yard in the United States with the main gun and machine gun removed. They were sold to farmers for agricultural use as well as to others. (US Army Signal Corps)

Egyptian service by 1948, via the British. Egyptian Locusts were used in the Arab-Israeli War, and three were captured by Israeli forces and used until 1953.

The M22 Locust light tank was the first and only tank designed and used for airborne operations during the Second World War. It had a low profile and a reasonably effective main gun using the Littlejohn squeeze-bore adapter. It suffered from rapid development and manufacturing without thorough testing. This led to several mechanical problems, especially with the transmission. When entering the battlefield fully functional, it performed as designed, assaulting German infantry units with firepower not usually associated with airborne operations. The M22 Locust light tank led the way for future development of airborne light tanks and suitable aircraft to deliver tanks to a battlefield.

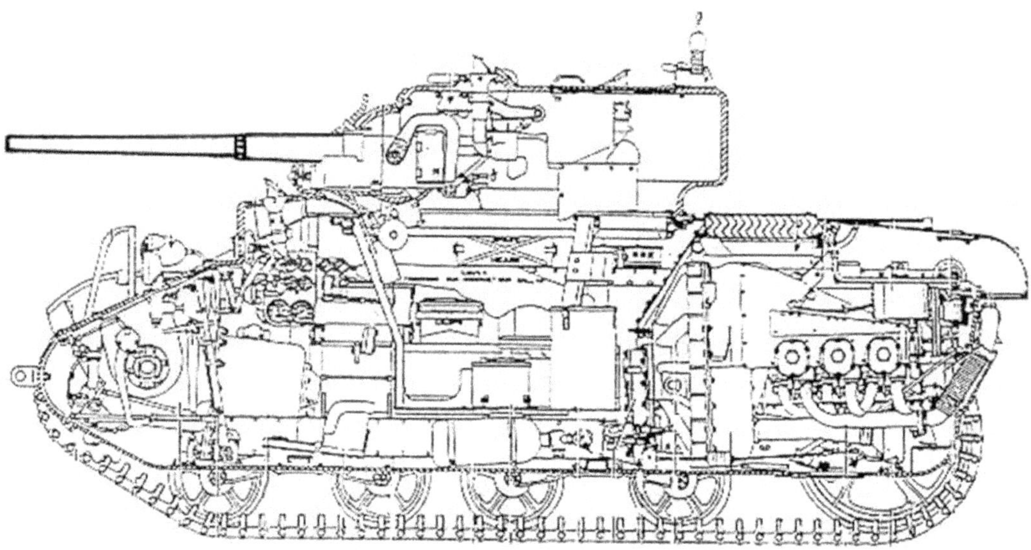

Appendix

151st Airborne Tank Company Daily Log

The source for this section is the US Army 151st Airborne Tank Company Unit Records, Dwight D. Eisenhower Presidential Library and Museum, Abilene, Kansas.

1943

15 Aug. 151st Airborne Tank Co., activated at Fort Knox, Kentucky, per GO #77, Hq Armored Command, dated 12 August 43. Original recruitment of 5 officers and 70 EM per SO #137, Hq 20th Armored Division, dated 14 August 1943.

28 Aug. 22 EM assigned per SO #146, par 1, Hq 20th Armored Division, dated 27 August 1943.

30 Aug. 1 EM assigned from Demonstration Regiment, Armored School, Fort Knox, Kentucky. 1 EM assigned from Instruction Regiment, Training Group, Armored School, Fort Knox, Kentucky.

31 Aug. 1 EM assigned from Demonstration Regiment, Armored School.

Strength as of 31 August 1943, 5 officers, 95 EM.

17 Nov. 1 EM discharged for Convenience of Government.

18 Nov. 1 WOJG assigned to Company.

26 Nov. 1 WOJG assigned 785th Tank Battalion, Fort Knox, Kentucky.

Strength as of 30 November 1943, 5 officers, 94 EM.

1 Dec. 1 EM assigned from ARTC, Fort Knox, Kentucky.

8 Dec. 3 officers assigned from the 28th Airborne Tank Battalion, Fort Knox, Kentucky.

11 Dec. 1 officer assigned to 28th Airborne Tank Battalion, Fort Knox, Kentucky.
1 officer assigned from 28th Airborne Tank Battalion, Fort Knox, Kentucky.

13 Dec. 2 officers assigned to 28th Airborne Tank Battalion, Fort Knox, Kentucky.

20 Dec. 3 EM assigned from ARTC, Fort Knox, Kentucky.

24 Dec. 1 officer and 1 EM assigned to 28th Airborne Tank Battalion., Fort Knox, Kentucky.
1 EM assigned from 28th Airborne Tank Battalion, Fort Knox, Kentucky.

Strength as of 31 December 1943, 5 officers, 98 EM.

1944

2 Jan. 3 EM assigned from Fort McDowell, Angel Island, California.

7 Jan. 1 EM assigned to 28th Airborne Tank Battalion, Fort Knox, Kentucky.

8 Jan. 1 EM assigned to 28th Airborne Tank Battalion, Fort Knox, Kentucky.

12 Jan. 1 EM assigned from 28th Airborne Tank Battalion, Fort Knox, Kentucky.

13 Jan. 1 EM assigned to Armored School, Fort Knox, Kentucky.

19 Jan. 1 officer assigned from ARTC, Fort Knox, Kentucky.

Strength as of 31 January 1944, six officers, 99 EM.

2 Feb. 2 EM assigned from Armored School, Fort Knox, Kentucky.

9 Feb. 1 officer assigned from the 28th Airborne Tank Battalion, Fort Knox, Kentucky.

10 Feb. 1 officer assigned to 28th Airborne Tank Battalion, Fort Knox, Kentucky.

14 Feb. 1 officer assigned from Armored Command.

17 Feb. 4 EM transferred to ARTC, Fort Knox, Kentucky, per SO #38, par 9, Hq Armored Command, Fort Knox, Kentucky, dated 14 February 1944.
1 EM transferred to Armored School, per SO #38, par 9, Hq Armored Command, dated 14 February 1944.

22 Feb. 3 EM transferred to Hq ARTC, Fort Knox, Kentucky.

Strength as of 29 February 1944, 7 officers, 93 EM.

20 Apr. 1 officer relieved from assignment per SO #93, ASF, dated 18 April 1944.

Strength as of 30 April 1944, 6 officers, 93 EM.

26 May — 29 EM assigned from ARTC, Fort Knox, Kentucky, per SO #122, Hq ARTC, dated 22 May 1944.

27 May — 8 EM assigned from Hq Armored School, Fort Knox, Kentucky, per SO #116 par 37, 66, 68, Hq Armored School, dated 16 May 1944.

29 May — 1 EM transferred to Parachute School, Ft Benning, Ga, SO #76, par 46, Hq Armored Center.

Strength as of 31 May 1944, Six (6) Officers, 129 EM.

8 Jun. — 220 attached unassigned from 126th Sep Tank Company, per SO #114, par 2, Hq 22d Corps, dated 7 June 1944.

13 Jun. — 1 EM (attached unassigned) transferred to Hq 2nd Army per SO #96, par 1, Hq 28th Airborne Tank Battalion, Fort Knox, Kentucky.

14 Jun. — 1 EM transferred from Parachute School.

16 Jun. — 1 EM (attached unassigned) transferred to 3652 SU, University of Illinois, Champagne, Illinois, per SO #24, par 2, Hq 151st Airborne Tank Company.

21 Jun. — 1 EM transferred to Engr OCS, Fort Belvoir, Virginia, per SO #153, par 10, Hq 2nd Army, dated 6 June 1944.

28 Jun. — 108 EM (attached unassigned) transferred to AGF Replacement Depot #1, Fort George E. Meade, Maryland, per SO #23, Hq 151st Airborne Tank Company, dated 27 June 1944. 1 EM (attached unassigned) transferred to Armored School, Fort Knox, Kentucky, per SO #120, par 5, Hq 22nd Corps, dated 23 June 1944.

Strength as of 30 June 1944, 6 officers, 238 EM.

12 Jul. — 16 EM (attached unassigned) transferred to 87th Infantry Division, Fort Jackson, South Carolina per SO #142, par 8, Hq 22nd Corps, dated 8 July 1944.

9 EM (attached unassigned) transferred to 14th Armored Division, Camp Campbell, Kentucky, per SO #142, par 8, Hq 22nd Corps, dated 8 July 1944.

2 EM (attached unassigned) transferred to 840th QM Gas Supply Company, Camp Chaffee, Arkansas, per SO #142, par 8, Hq 22nd Corps, dated 8 July 1944.

1 EM (attached unassigned) transferred to 60th Signal Radio Int. Company, Camp Crowder, Missouri per SO #142, par 8, Hq 22nd Corps, dated 8 July 1944.

1 EM (attached unassigned) transferred to 97th Chem Battalion, Fort Lenard Wood, Missouri, per SO #142, par 8, Hq 22nd Corps, dated 8 July 1944.

14 Jul. 64 EM (attached unassigned) transferred to 87th Infantry Division, per SO #142 par 8, Hq 22nd Corps, dated 8 July 1944.

17 Jul. 16 EM (attached unassigned) transferred to 28th Airborne Tank Battalion, Fort Knox, Kentucky, per SO #147, par 5, Hq 22nd Corps, dated 13 July 1944.

Left Fort Knox, Kentucky, for Camp Mackall, North Carolina, on permanent change of station.

19 Jul. Arrived at Camp Mackall, North Carolina.

20 Jul. 73 EM assigned en route from Armored Replacement Training Center, Fort Knox, Kentucky, per SO #165, par 12, Hq ARTC.

22 Jul. 4 EM transferred to 16th Armored Division, Camp Chaffe, Arkansas, per SO #31, par 2, Hq 151st Airborne Tank Company.

3 EM transferred to 13th Armored Division, Camp Bowie, Texas, per SO #31, par 3, Hq 151st Airborne Tank Company.

1 EM assigned from 1112 SU, Fort Devens, Massachusetts, 23 July, per So #175, par 5, Headquarters SCU 1112, Fort Devens, Massachusetts, dated 22 July 1944.

Strength as of 31 July 1944, 6 officers, 196 EM.

7 Aug. 9 EM assigned from The Armored School, Fort Knox, Kentucky, per SO #181 par 49, Hq TAS, dated 31 July 1944.

8 Aug. 13 EM transferred to 12th Armored Division, Camp Barkeley, Texas, per SO #35, par 2, Hq 151st Airborne Tank Company, dated 4 August 1944.

10 Aug. 1 officer assigned to Parachute School, Fort Benning, Georgia.

14 Aug. 1 EM transferred to 542 Parachute Infantry Battalion, Camp Mackall, North Carolina, per SO #87, par 1, Hq Airborne Center, Camp Mackall, North Carolina.

18 Aug. 2 EM transferred to 71st Infantry Division, Fort Benning, Georgia, per SO #88, par 3, Hq Airborne Center, Camp Mackall, North Carolina.

22 Aug. 9 EM assigned per SO #181, par 49, Hq TAS, are dropped from rolls Per TWX, Hq ASF, authority GNACR 3378.

Strength as of 30 September 1944, 5 officers, 180 EM.

1 Sep. 5 officers and 171 EM complete Glider Training and Qualified as Gliderman per SO #101, par 3 Hq Airborne Center, Camp Mackall, North Carolina, dated 1 September 1944.

3 EM transferred to 37th Infantry Division, Fort Benning, Georgia, per SO #98, par 1 Hq Airborne Center, Camp Mackall, North Carolina.

4 Sep. 1 EM transferred to 37th Infantry Regiment, Fort Benning, Georgia, SO #101, par 1, Hq Airborne Center, Camp Mackall, North Carolina.

14 Sep. 1 EM AWOL from 14 August 1944 dropped from rolls.

15 Sep. 1 EM transferred to ASF Regional Hospital, Fort Bragg, North Carolina, per SO #222, par 6, Hq Camp Mackall, North Carolina.

29 Sep. 1 EM transferred to ASF Regional Hospital, per SO #235, par 8, Hq Camp Mackall, North Carolina.

Strength as of 30 September 1944, 5 officers, 173 EM.

Participated in Airborne Maneuvers, Camp Mackall, North Carolina, per VOCO, Airborne Center, dated 24 September–6 October 1944.

6 Oct. 1 EM desertion to hands of Military Authorities, Camp Butner, North Carolina.

31 Oct. 1 EM transferred to 469th QM Depot Company, Camp Shelby, Missouri, SO #128, par 2, Headquarters, Airborne Center.

Strength as of 31 October 1944, 5 officers, 173 EM.

3 Nov. 1 EM transferred to AAF Basic Training Center, Keesler Field, Biloxi, Missouri, per SO #130, par 1, Hq Airborne Center.

19 Nov. 1 EM transferred to Separation Center, 1st Service Command, Fort Devens, Massachusetts, per SO #143, par 3, Hq Airborne Center.

20 Nov. 1 EM transferred to 259th AGF Band, Fort Riley, Kansas, per SO #143, par 3 Hq Airborne Center.

23 Nov. 2 EM transferred to 37th Infantry Regiment, Fort Benning, Georgia, per SO #127, par 3, Headquarters, Airborne Center.

1 EM transferred to 37th Infantry Regiment, Fort Benning, Georgia., per SO #137, par 2, Headquarters, Airborne Center.

Strength as of 30 November 1944, 5 officers, 167 EM.

7 Dec. 1 EM transferred to Parachute School, Fort Benning, Georgia, per SO #132, par 2, Headquarters, Airborne Center.

9 Dec. 1 EM transferred to Separation Center, 6th SC, Fort Sheridan, Illinois, per SO #153, par 3, Hq Airborne Center.

11 Dec. 1 EM transferred to Separation Center, 2nd Service Command, Fort Dix, New Jersey per SO #155, par 2, Hq Airborne Center.

12 Dec. 1 EM transferred to Separation Center, 4th Service Command, Fort Sam Houston, Texas, per SO #155, par 3, Hq Airborne Center.

15 Dec. 1 EM Confinement to 1495th Service Unit, Camp Mackall, North Carolina, per GCMO #108, Hq 13th Airborne Division, Camp Mackall, North Carolina, dated 9 December 1944.

16 Dec. 1 EM transferred to AAF Basic Training Center, Keesler Field, Missouri, per SO #158, par 1, Hq Airborne Center.

20 Dec. 8 EM transferred to 13th Armored Division, Camp Bowie, Texas, per SO #161, par 1, Headquarters, Airborne Center.

23 Dec. 2 EM transferred to Airborne Board, Camp Mackall, North Carolina, per SO #165, par 3, Headquarters, Airborne Center.

1 EM transferred to Hq and Hq Company, Airborne Center, Camp Mackall, North Carolina, per SO #165, par 2 Hq Airborne Center.

27 Dec. 13 EM transferred to 13th Armored Division, Camp Bowie, Texas, per SO 165, par 4, Hq Airborne Center.

Strength as of 28 December 1944, 5 officers, 137 EM.

31 Dec. 5 officers relieved from assignment and assigned to Armored Officers replacement Pool, Fort Knox, Kentucky per par 1 SO #168, Hq Airborne Center 27 Dec. 1944.

120 EM transferred to AGF Replacement Depot #1, per par 4, SO 170, 30 December 1944.

1 EM transferred to Hq Company, Airborne Center, per par 2, SO 170, Hq Airborne Center, dated 30 December 1944.

16 EM transferred to AGF Replacement Depot #1, per par 6, SO 170 dated 30 December 1944.

Strength as of 2400 31 December 1944, Zero officers and Zero EM.

Recommended Reading

Air Progress Magazine, Byrd Aviation Books, 114 Deer Path Road, Williamsburg, Virginia

Harclerode, Peter. *Go To It, the Illustrated History of the 6th Airborne Division*, Claxton Edition, 2000

Hunnicut, R.P. *Stuart, A History of the American Light Tank*, Presidio Press, 1992

Icks, Robert J. *Light Tanks M22 Locust and M24 Chaffee*, Profile Publications Ltd, 1972

TM 9-1724A, *Engine and Engine Accessories for Light Tank T9E1*, War Department, August 1943

Zaloga, Steven J. *M551 Sheridan: U.S. Airmobile Tanks 1941–2001*, Osprey Publishing, 2009